BIG AGENDA

BIG AGENDA

President Trump's Plan to Save America

DAVID HOROWITZ

Humanix Books

Big Agenda

Humanix Books, P.O. Box 20989, West Palm Beach, FL 33416, USA
www.humanixbooks.com | info@humanixbooks.com

Library of Congress Control Number: 2016958781

Cover Photo: Alamy, FHYP6R
Interior Design: Scribe Inc.

Humanix Books is a division of Humanix Publishing, LLC. Its trademark, consisting of the word "Humanix," is registered in the Patent and Trademark Office and in other countries.

ISBN: 978-1-63006-087-9 (Hardcover)
ISBN: 978-1-63006-088-6 (E-book)

Printed in the United States of America
10 9 8 7 6 5 4 3 2

Freedom is never more than one generation away from extinction. We didn't pass it to our children in the bloodstream. It must be fought for, protected, and handed on for them to do the same.

—Ronald Reagan

Contents

Introduction

Restoring the Nation to Greatness

Donald Trump's victory in the 2016 election was a political earthquake. It put an end to eight years of a left-wing presidency that divided the American people, eroded American sovereignty, diminished American power, and undermined a constitutional foundation that had made America prosperous and great.

Before the election, conservatives were justifiably worried that America's decline was reaching a point of no return. When the results came in, they breathed a sigh of relief. A long and arduous battle had been successfully concluded. With conservatives in control of the three branches of government, the groundwork was laid to restore the country to prosperity and health. Americans could roll up their sleeves and begin the hard work of restoring the nation to greatness again.

There was truth in this feeling, but it was only a partial truth. To begin with, the election was narrowly won. Half the country had voted for a candidate who vowed to continue the Obama administration policies that had brought the nation to the brink. Half the country had voted for a candidate in favor of open borders, a candidate who willingly prosecuted the gender and racial wars of the political left. Half the country had voted for a candidate who viewed the Constitution as a changeable document, a candidate ready to appoint Supreme Court justices who believed its decisions should be based not on the law but on whether they achieved a progressive result.

When the votes were in, the anguished voices of the left provided a foretaste of the future in store for Republicans and their president over the next four years. "Mourning in America" was the way the *Huffington Post* announced Trump's victory on the day after the election.[1] "President Trump: A Colossal Failure for Democracy, and Our Terrifying New Reality," responded Salon.com, a website owned by the *Washington Post*.[2] Stoking the fires of racial conflict, CNN's Van Jones called the election "a white-lash against a black president."[3] Echoing the incitement, Slate.com, owned by Microsoft, declared: "White Won." This was *Slate*'s headline for a story by Jamelle Bouie, which read: "Trump promised a resurgent white supremacy. And white voters embraced it. We are still the country that produced George Wallace. We are still the country that killed Emmet Till."[4] As if ginning up a race war wasn't sufficient, *Slate* also ran an article with the headline "I Am a Gay Jew in Trump's America. And I Am Afraid for My Life."[5]

These emotional provocations reflect the passions of a left that would not be stilled by the election result or conciliatory gestures the new president had already made. Instead, they will be inflamed by every step Trump takes along the path to reviving a battered country and restoring its constitutional order. These are the angry voices of a political culture that is at war with America. Worse yet, this is the dominant culture in our universities, in our media, in our judiciary, in government unions, and in the shadow political universe of nonprofits, with billions of tax-free dollars at their disposal.

The late Andrew Breitbart wisely observed that "politics is downstream from culture." The culture wars conservatives have lost over the last half-century have transformed the Democratic Party into a party of the left and have led to the eight-year tenure of a radical president. These are the wars that must still be fought and won if the election victory is to remain secure; these are the wars that must be fought and won to keep the country back from the brink.

One battle is over, but there are many more to come. This book is a guide to fighting the opponents of the conservative restoration. It identifies who the adversaries are—their methods and their motivations. It describes their agenda—not merely the particular issues with which they advance their goal, but the destructive goal itself. And it lays out a strategy that can defeat them.

PART I

THE ADVERSARY

1

New Wars to Fight

As we enter the Trump era, our country faces daunting threats to its security, prosperity, and freedom. For eight years, we have been led by a commander-in-chief dedicated to appeasing our enemies and degrading our military, reducing its forces to their lowest level since World War II. Weakness and uncertain resolve by America's commander-in-chief have led to an expanding terrorist threat abroad and increasing terrorist attacks at home. At home, overtaxation, overregulation, and massive government debt have led to the most anemic economic recovery on record. Ninety-four million Americans have left the work force, and 47 million are on food stamps. Thirty years of Democratic Party attacks on our sovereignty have created porous national borders and an influx of hundreds of thousands of criminals and an unknown number of terrorists. Hundreds of Democrat-sponsored "Sanctuary Cities"—including such major urban centers as Los Angeles and New York—have set precedents of sedition by defying federal law to provide safe havens for criminals and terrorists who have crossed our borders illegally. Once-eradicated epidemic diseases like tuberculosis have returned with the influx of refugees from Somalia and other war-torn Third World countries, while our left-wing government has been busy importing tens of thousands of unvetted refugees from Middle-Eastern centers of the Islamic holy war against us.

At home, another war with racial overtones is being waged by the left and directed at law enforcement in cities across America, leading to a dramatic spike in homicides and other violent crimes. Aggressive assaults by progressives on the First and Second Amendments—the cornerstones of America's freedoms—have divided America's communities and set precedents for drastic curtailments of other American freedoms. Today, America is more divided and its major parties more polarized than at any time since the Civil War. The conclusion of the nastiest, most divisive election campaign within living memory augurs little hope that these conflicts will not occupy center stage in the political dramas of the next four years.

2

Divisions on the Right

DIVISIONS HAVE OPENED UP within the parties as well. But it is the division within the Republican Party that should be the first concern of Americans disturbed by the radicalism of the Obama years. Although Republicans finally "came home" to provide Trump with his margin of victory, a cohort of "Never Trumpers" did not. In 2012, the party's nominee, Mitt Romney, had avidly sought Trump's endorsement, saying, "Donald Trump has shown an extraordinary ability to understand how our economy works to create jobs for the American people. He's done it here in Nevada. He's done it across the country. . . . I spent my life in the private sector. Not quite as successful as this guy."[1] But in 2016, when his country's future was on the line, Romney led renegade

Republicans in sabotaging the party's nominee: "Here's what I know: Donald Trump is a phony, a fraud."[2] Romney's eruption, like many similar attacks from "Never Trumpers," was hard to explain. Romney certainly had never said anything as harsh about Obama during the 2012 campaign. Predictably, Democrats featured his outburst, along with those of several other disgruntled Republicans, in attack ads against a candidate who had won more primary votes than any Republican in history.

Former presidents George Herbert Walker Bush and George W. Bush sat on their hands throughout the campaign while making their displeasure with the candidate clear. A month before the November election, defeated primary candidate Jeb Bush pronounced Trump beyond the pale over an 11-year-old video that had been released by the pro-Clinton *Washington Post* in an effort to derail the Republican's campaign. The video showed the candidate talking boorishly in a private conversation with Jeb's cousin Billy.[3] Trump apologized for his remarks, but Bush refused to accept his apology. "As the grandfather of two precious girls," he tweeted, "I find that no apology can excuse away Donald Trump's reprehensible comments degrading women."[4] This denial of forgiveness to Trump seemed somewhat inexplicable given the Bush family's well-known embrace of Bill Clinton, whose sexual abuses, unlike Trump's, were actions rather than boasts in private and were committed by a sitting governor and president and then exposed in front of a whole nation of precious girls.[5]

Claiming to be outraged by the video, as well as by other casual Trump remarks, some former members of the George W.

Bush White House went so far as to announce that they were voting for the Democrat, Hillary Clinton. A former policy director for the House Republican conference, Evan McMullin, even launched a presidential run in Utah in the hopes of blocking a Trump majority in the Electoral College. All these defections raise troubling questions: What was it that these Republicans didn't understand about the Democrats and their responsibility for the present perils of the nation? What did they not understand about the destructive agendas of the left that threatened its future?

Were these "Never Trumpers" intimidated by the massive barrage of baseless, malicious, and overblown attacks on the candidate's character, which permeated the media and the culture at large? Or did they withdraw simply because they lacked the stomach for the fight? One prominent conservative concluded that they simply didn't have the will to win. "The Republican Party is not interested in winning," Rush Limbaugh told the millions in his radio audience.

> It clearly is not interested in winning. And if you want to be even more specific than that, it is paramountly obvious that they're not even interested in defeating the Democrats. It's just mind-boggling. All of these years I've been doing this program I was under the impression the Republican Party wanted to beat Democrats. And as the years have gone by, it's become obvious to me that that's not their No. 1 objective. We have Republicans—to one degree or another—working as hard as the Democrats are to defeat Donald Trump. The country we know and love is being torn apart and rebuilt in ways that we don't want, and the Republican Party doesn't even seem to

> care about that. The Republican Party seems just as eager as the Democrats to pronounce their voters as extreme kooks.[6]

Here Limbaugh was echoing a populist theme of Trump's campaign—that a political class had rigged the system. As both men argued, the problem was not a flawed *candidate* but a failed *party*. The loss of nerve that had handcuffed the Republican opposition to Obama's second term was not restricted to the Republican leadership. Republicans generally didn't understand the threat posed by the Democrats or didn't have the will to resist it—or both. It was a failure of nerve by the entire party, which, despite landslide victories that had given them their biggest majority in the House in nearly 100 years, would not use their power to block Obama's socialist agendas.

3

The Roots of Executive Tyranny

THE SIGNIFICANCE OF A House majority lies in the role the Constitution assigns to this chamber. The founders were concerned about the chief executive they had created and the possibility that an unscrupulous occupant of the White House might attempt to make himself a new monarch. They were concerned that, like Obama, he might spurn the legislative powers of Congress and rule by executive order. As Andrew McCarthy explained in an article for *National Review*, the Constitution entrusted the House with two checks on an executive tyranny.[1] The first lay in the power of the purse, which the House could use to block any expansion of executive power by denying the president the means to achieve it. They could defund his unconstitutional programs and remove the means to execute his extralegal designs. The second check was impeachment, available when the president proved so lawless as to require removal.

But when Obama acted illegally, legislating changes in Obamacare from the executive branch and granting amnesty to illegal aliens that he himself conceded were unauthorized, the majorities elected by Republican voters failed to employ either of the constitutional checks to stop him. During the 2014 campaign, Senate Majority Leader Mitch McConnell assured Republicans that their elected representatives would use the congressional purse to block the Obama agenda: "In the spending bill we will be pushing back against this bureaucracy by doing what's called placing riders in the bill. No money can be spent to do this or to do that [without congressional approval]. We're going to go after them on health care, on financial services, on the Environmental Protection Agency, across the board. All across the federal government, we're going to go after it."[2]

But then, as McCarthy notes, the Republicans won the election, "and they agree[d] to pay for everything they campaigned against—Obamacare, immigration lawlessness, a Justice Department that practices racial discrimination in law-enforcement while using extortionate lawsuits to federalize the nation's police, an IRS used as a weapon against conservative activists, an EPA decreeing economy-strangling regulations Congress has refused to enact, and so on. Moreover, they pass[ed] sleight-of-hand legislation to duck confrontations with Obama on the debt ceiling and the Iran deal—pieces of theater designed to dismantle the Constitution's brakes but to allow them to pose as opposing that which their legislation actually enables."[3] The result of the Republicans' cowardice was the breakdown of the constitutional system, the disenfranchisement of Republican voters, the establishment of an executive tyranny, and the continuing corruption of government institutions like the IRS and the Departments of Justice and Homeland Security. The result was a government growing ever more abusive and intrusive, able to expand its powers over a people whose will it could disregard without consequence.

The fecklessness of their leaders produced enough frustration and rage in the Republican ranks to produce the candidacy of an outsider, an American patriot distressed by the state of corruption and decline into which his country had fallen. Donald Trump's blunt exposure of the rigged nature of the system, his willingness to disregard the politically correct constraints on public discourse, and his readiness to relentlessly attack the culprits struck a profound chord with record numbers of Republicans reacting to years of frustration and disappointment. The passions Trump aroused in the electorate sparked a revolt in the Republican Party and allowed him, as a political novice, to defeat 16 seasoned and tested rivals in the Republican primaries.

The failure of the Republican House to use its power to check Obama's lawlessness and prevent his ever-expanding intrusions into the lives of Americans is easily understood. Republicans were afraid of being called "obstructionists" by the Democratic political machine and its media extensions. They were afraid of being stigmatized as "heartless" or "racist" or "xenophobic" when Democrats picked items out of the omnibus budget bill that provided aid to minorities or the poor or children. They were impotent because they did not have a political response to these Democratic attacks—nothing that would neutralize the powerful emotional appeal to voters from pleas on behalf of society's defenseless and vulnerable. This gaping deficit in the conservative arsenal is manifest every time a Republican squares off with a Democrat, goes on the defensive, and then folds in the face of an overwhelming assault.[4]

4

The Progressive Movement

How can Republicans close the gap? How can they come up with a strategy for neutralizing the Democrats' attacks and putting them on the defensive? How can conservatives stop the Democratic Party's drive to dismantle the constitutional foundations of the nation and reshape its social order?

To answer these questions, Republicans and conservatives first need to know exactly who their adversaries are. That means not just Hillary Clinton or Tim Kaine or Bernie Sanders but the progressive movement they have committed their political lives to advancing. What are the motivations of the millions of Americans who are part of this movement? What are their methods and long-term goals? What is their agenda?

In the first place, this is not just a matter of specific policies and programs any more than it is a movement advanced by individual leaders of the Democratic Party. It is a matter of the powerful, almost religious convictions of the progressive movement. This movement is too powerful inside and outside the Democratic Party for an individual leader to deviate too far from the progressive path. Individual policies and programs are but the tips of the iceberg; what you see is not what you eventually get, for policies and programs can be—and are—tailored to the political moment, then abandoned and revived in more radical forms. Obamacare is a prime example. As Republicans long suspected, it was designed by its architects to fail so that after laying the groundwork for socialized medicine, they could expand Obamacare with a "single-payer" plan—that is, total government control of the nation's health.[1]

What is important is not the specific policy but the *ideology* behind the policy, the long-term vision that a policy like Obamacare is the instrumental means of achieving. Republicans will agree that the failure to name our adversary in the so-called war on terror is a severe—possibly even fatal—handicap when it comes to defeating the enemy. But this is also true of political conflicts. Without understanding the motivations and intentions of one's adversaries, it is difficult—perhaps impossible—to defeat them. For half a century now, conservatives have been mainly losing the political and culture wars with the left because they do not understand what their adversaries are up to—what drives them and shapes their means and ends.

So we must begin with that. When we set out to defend our country and its constitutional framework, whom are we up against? What is the inspirational goal that underlies their calculations and justifies their deeds? How do they see *us*? What are they prepared to do to defeat us? What laws will they break, what deceptions will they employ, and what acts will they commit? How many conservatives prior to this election year and the WikiLeaks document dumps would have expected that the Clintons were capable of so many criminal acts and such contempt for the safety of ordinary Americans?

An answer to the question "How do they see us?" was provided by Donald Trump during the second presidential debate. The answer was so harsh in its judgment it was probably unprecedented in the annals of modern presidential politics. Trump turned to the audience at one point to say, "Hillary has tremendous hatred in her heart." It was the kind of politically incorrect character description that had become a signature reflex of Trump's election campaign. Never before had one presidential candidate so bluntly confronted another. Never had *any* Republican dared to characterize a Democratic opponent in such damning moral terms to a national audience. Pre-Trump Republicans were generally too polite to blurt out such conclusions even when they were just.

The same cannot be said for Democrats or Hillary. It was Hillary who provided the occasion for Trump's remark. His judgment of Hillary's character did not come out of the blue. It was a direct response to the attacks that had been the focus of her campaign. It was really her core message, which was a vicious and personal attempt to condemn Trump and his supporters as "unfit" to lead the country. The trigger of Trump's remark was a statement she had made on the campaign trail and had not retracted. Addressing an LGBTQ event a month earlier, Clinton had dismissed Trump's supporters out of hand. In as casual a way as one could make such dehumanizing comments, Clinton had said that half of Trump's supporters belonged in her "basket of deplorables," then added that they were "irredeemable." Nor did she leave these characterizations hanging in the air for others to imagine what she could have meant by such remarks. Instead, she rattled off an itemized list to clarify exactly what she had in mind: "You know, to just be grossly generalistic, you could put half of Trump's supporters into what I call the basket of deplorables. Right? The racist, sexist, homophobic, xenophobic, Islamophobic—you name it. And unfortunately there are people like that. And he has lifted them up."[2] Reaffirming this demonization of Republicans and their candidate right to the end of the campaign, both Hillary and Obama suggested in ads and appearances that Trump was the candidate of the Ku Klux Klan.[3]

Out of the other side of her mouth, Hillary regularly invoked her "favorite quote" from Michelle Obama: "When they go low, we go high." Closer to the truth would have been "When they go low, we go lower."

Of course, such demonizing epithets are hardly peculiar to Hillary Clinton, nor is the reflexive damning of those who disagree with her. These are the familiar anathemas of the politically correct deployed against people whose opinions they don't like. What her "deplorable" remark tells us is that Hillary Clinton is not alone in having tremendous hatred in her heart for Republicans and for all those who do not share her political views. What the anathemas tell us is that Democrats, and progressives generally, harbor the same hatred for their political opponents. Republicans don't really need to be told this, since they have ample personal confirmations. What Republican has not had these same hateful words applied to them by a Democratic opponent?

5

The Race Card

EVERY ELECTION CYCLE, DEMOCRATS run campaigns against Republicans, accusing them of being racist, of wanting to put blacks in chains (as Vice President Joe Biden so crudely charged during the 2012 election). Nor is it just Democratic *politicians* who think this way. In arguments with progressives over what might have seemed simple policy disagreements, what conservative has *not* had the unpleasant experience of being called a racist, sexist, homophobe, xenophobe, or Islamophobe? If you think America should have secure borders and a legal process for immigration, as every other nation does—Mexico in particular—you are immediately in danger of having a progressive label you "anti-immigrant," "racist," and "xenophobic" (if they know the word). That is how progressives and Democrats talk, and that is how they think.

In the second debate, Hillary actually called Trump a "racist," which is probably also unprecedented in presidential debates. "He has really started his political activity," she said, "based on this racist lie that our first black president was not an American citizen."[1] This was a reference to Trump's role in pressuring Obama to produce his birth certificate, something Obama had resisted doing two years into his presidency. The issue spoke to his qualifications to be president, since the Constitution stipulates that the president has to be American by birth. Since Obama was notorious for playing fast and loose with the truth, in particular for making up "facts" about his biography, and since his father was a Kenyan national, this was hardly an unreasonable question to pursue.[2] Nor would a suggestion that Obama was not an American citizen fall into the category of "lie," let alone "racist." Trump continued his pursuit after questions were raised by others about the birth certificate Obama produced. That was unwise, but Trump's rejoinder to Clinton was to point out that it was she herself who had originated the so-called birther claim in her 2008 primary fight with Obama. Her own campaign strategist in 2016 conceded that this was true and that she had indeed attempted to show that Obama was not an American by birth.[3] In other words, the birther claim only became "racist" when raised by a Republican.

It is particularly significant that these charges of racism not only against Trump but against Republicans generally come at a time when America has driven the racists who still exist underground—or at least the *white* racists. What public figure can reasonably be called an antiblack racist other than the universally condemned David Duke? Far from being racists, Americans are generally the most tolerant people on the planet, certainly in comparison to any other country with large minority communities. William H. Frey of the Brookings Institution points out these statistics: "Sociologists have traditionally viewed multiracial marriage as a benchmark for the ultimate assimilation of a particular group into society. Black-white marriages were still illegal in 16 states until 1967. And a 1958 Gallup poll found that only 4% of Americans approved of black-white marriages. Today that number is 87%. In 1960, of all marriages by blacks, only 1.7% were black-white. Today it's 12% and rising."[4] Orlando Patterson is a renowned liberal Harvard sociologist with award-winning works on the study of slavery and race. Patterson is also black, but in his judgment, America "is the least racist white-majority society in the world; has a better record of legal protections of minorities than any other society, white or black; [and] offers more opportunities to greater numbers of black persons than any other society, including those of Africa."[5]

This is the reality, yet Democrats like Hillary Clinton and Barack Obama regard America as "systemically racist" and deploy the race card as a political weapon every chance that presents itself. If it is evident that American society is not racist, why are these accusations against Republicans and conservatives so common as to be almost predictable? They are predictable because they are effective in marginalizing and discrediting opponents of the progressive agenda. And they are effective because Republicans, with rare exceptions like

Donald Trump, have no effective response—no counterattack—to neutralize them.

The real effect of calling people racists is to drum them out of the company of decent people and to stigmatize them as "extremists," social outcasts, and unsuitable to participate in any legitimate conversation. It is because America is *not* a racist society that there is an American consensus that racists—or at least white racists—are hateful. If Democrats call you a racist because you are a conservative or a Republican, that tells you that you are *hated* because you are a conservative or a Republican; you are irredeemable and belong in the "basket of deplorables."

6

Hatred in Their Hearts

THE CHIEF STRATEGY OF Democratic political campaigns is to use character assassination, otherwise referred to as "the politics of personal destruction," as the weapon of choice. Any strategy for resisting these attacks has to begin with an understanding of this brutal fact. The first requirement for any strategy to stop their progressive agenda is to understand that they have tremendous hatred in their hearts for those who oppose them. The second requirement is to know how to confound that hatred. If your opponents are prepared to demonize you as a racist and you have no equally powerful response, you might as well quit the field of battle.

Why *do* progressives have hatred in their hearts for conservatives? Why do they sound like hellfire-and-damnation preachers when they are on the attack? Because they are zealots of what can only be described as a crypto-religion modeled on the Christian narrative of the Fall and Redemption—the difference being that they see themselves as the redeemers instead of the divinity. To progressives, the world is a fallen place—beset by racism, sexism, homophobia, and the rest—that must be transformed and made right. This redemption was once called communism and is now called socialism, or "social justice." Theirs is a vision of a world that has become a "safe place"—where there are no deplorables, or where such irredeemables are outlawed and suppressed.

Progressives dream of a world of political correctness and politically enforced equality, where everybody is taken care of by taxing the rich until there are no more rich, universities and schools admit no ideas that are hurtful or offending, environments have no pollution, countries have no borders, and nations have no armies. Progressives are so enthralled by their dreams of a heaven on earth that they see those who oppose their dreams as evil, which is why they hate them. For what decent soul would be against a world in which everyone was taken care of, guaranteed a "living wage," and provided with free education and health care, food and housing—a world in which all needs are met and there is social justice? What decent person could oppose the idea of open borders that would recognize all the diverse people in the world as part of one big human family? It's a beautiful dream, and to one degree or another every progressive shares it. Progressives are social redeemers. They see themselves as saving the vulnerable and saving the planet. Consequently, they regard themselves as the army of the saints and those who oppose them as the party of the damned.

This is why Democrats go forward in lockstep while Republicans march to the beat of their own drums. Closing ranks is almost an instinct with Democrats, while solidarity in the line of fire helps them prevail in political battles. How much of an instinct is the lockstep mentality displayed by progressives? Consider one pivotal moment in the recent election campaign—the moment when the polls took a dramatic turn against Trump after an 11-year-old "sex-talk video" was unearthed by the pro-Clinton *Washington Post.* Democrats responded across the board with outrage, much of it bizarre considering what Democrats—Hollywood Democrats in particular—regularly put up with when sex talk and abusive behavior appears in their own ranks. This particular revelation triggered an immediate exodus of Republicans announcing they could not support their party's candidate and would not be part of his campaign. It was a bridge too far. "I am sickened by what I heard today," Speaker Paul Ryan said in a statement notable for its political correctness, as he boycotted a Trump event. "Women are to be championed and revered, not objectified."[1]

Now try to name one Democrat who defected because they were sickened or appalled by something their candidate actually *did*, as opposed to merely said. Hillary Clinton violated the espionage laws; she broke her oaths of office; she lied to Congress and the FBI about her illegal server, which exposed classified secrets to America's enemies; she lied to the general public to hide what she did and repeated her lies over the course of a year; she lied about the number of illegal, unsecure handheld devices she used, and she destroyed or "lost" all of them to hide what she had done; she obstructed justice—a felony—by destroying her e-mails days after Congress had subpoenaed them and warned her *not* to destroy them; she lied to the American public and the world about the deaths of four American heroes, including an ambassador who was her friend and whose demise came about as a result of circumstances in which she had played a significant role; she lied to the mothers of the dead over their coffins. Yet through all this disgraceful and criminal activity, which would have disqualified anyone else as a presidential candidate, not a single Democratic elected official—not one—said, "This is a bridge too far; I can't go along with her on this." Not one.

Why not? Because she was their candidate and, more important, the standard bearer of the progressive cause; because they were going into an election that would shape the nation's future and advance the cause of social justice. Because breaking ranks would be giving aid to the enemy, to those who oppose the beautiful dream: the racists and sexists, the deplorables.

7

No Rules for Radicals

Another way to look at this progressive worldview is to understand the origins and uses of "political correctness." *Political correctness* is actually a term coined by the Chinese dictator and mass murderer Mao Zedong. By "politically correct," Mao meant adhering to the official position of the Communist Party, which the comrades referred to as "the party line." Those who deviated from the party line, who expressed views that were politically incorrect, were guilty of betraying the communist dream and therefore of betraying the oppressed. For their betrayal, they were subjected to disciplinary measures and expulsion, which meant the loss not only of their party affiliation but of their community of friends and comrades. Although progressives in America are not communists in the Maoist sense, being politically incorrect in their ranks also entails punishment and shaming. If the offense is great enough, it can mean expulsion from progressive communities that include virtually all of one's friends. This is a crucial reason why progressives don't break ranks the way conservatives do.

The party line creates the solidarity, the lockstep, that is crucial to winning political battles and achieving the cherished goal: communism for Mao, "social justice" for progressives. Political correctness embodies and enforces the worldview of the party, which sees itself as the vanguard of the vulnerable and oppressed. Like their leftist predecessors, progressives see the world as divided into the haves and the have-nots, the 1 percent and the 99 percent, the victimizers and the victims, the powerful and the rest. Maintaining the party line—being politically correct—puts one in the vanguard of social progress. Deviating from the party line is the betrayal of this trust and rightly risks expulsion from the progressive community. It means joining the ranks of the deplorables. It means being shunned. If you are a progressive, the last thing you want to be called is a racist, a sexist, an Islamophobe, or a Republican.

Hillary Clinton and Barack Obama, and progressives generally, are disciples of the political organizer Saul Alinsky, whose *Rules for Radicals* has provided a well-thumbed guidebook for the contemporary left. This book has pride of place on the recommended reading list of the nation's largest teachers union, the National Education Association.[1] Obama was trained as an Alinsky organizer and for decades worked with Alinsky organizations and activists to achieve radical goals.[2] When Hillary was an undergraduate at Wellesley in

1969, she interviewed Alinsky and devoted her senior thesis to his theories and achievements. She compared him to Eugene Debs, Walt Whitman, and Martin Luther King Jr. and portrayed him as an American hero.

Alinsky regarded himself as a revolutionary leftist and embraced the Marxist view that society was divided into haves and have-nots, oppressors and oppressed. To achieve equality and justice required Machiavellian means. "*The Prince* was written by Machiavelli for the Haves on how to hold power," Alinsky explained. "*Rules for Radicals* is written for the Have-Nots on how to take it away."[3] There was no room in Alinsky's leftist worldview for the recognition that there are also "can-dos" and "can-nots" and "will-dos and will-nots" or that in a capitalist society there is mobility both upward and downward.

Tactically speaking, Alinsky was critical of the way sixties' radicals went about trying to accomplish their ends. In particular, he was upset at the way they telegraphed their agendas and were frank about their goals. "We want a revolution, and we want it now!" was a typical radical slogan of the time. Alinsky was critical of sixties' activists who shouted slogans to "Burn the system down!" Of them, he said, "They have no illusions about the system, but plenty of illusions about the way to change our world. It is to this point that I have written this book."[4] Alinsky was not appalled that sixties' radicals wanted to burn the American system down; he was appalled that they would communicate that desire to the public. Being candid about their agendas, he wrote, would turn off potential recruits, create resistance, and make it impossible for them to achieve their goal. He was particularly distressed by the way they attacked the Democratic Party, which was the party of labor and the vehicle through which he thought they could actually achieve power. The advice his book offers to future radicals is this: lie about your intentions and join the Democratic Party; once inside the Democratic Party, you can subvert America's institutions from within.

The most important chapter of Alinsky's guide is called "Means and Ends" and is designed to address Alinsky's biggest problem: how to explain to radicals who think they are creating a world of justice and harmony that the means they must use to get there are Machiavellian—deceitful, conniving, brutal, and ruthless. Alinsky answers the question with a statement worthy of the famous question Pontius Pilate put to Jesus: "What is truth?" The progressive organizer, he writes, "does not have a fixed truth—truth to him is relative and changing; *everything* to him is relative and changing. He is a political relativist."[5] Or a nihilist. Judging by the events of the election year alone, Hillary Clinton would qualify as a model Alinsky disciple.

The Alinsky activist breaks the rules whenever doing so advances the progressive cause. Being an activist in the service of the higher good becomes a license to do anything required to achieve that good. The ends justify the means. But this raises the question of whether one can create a new world—a world that is socially just—by belonging to a political movement that is corrupt. Alinsky dismisses any such concern: "To say that corrupt means corrupt the ends is to believe in the immaculate conception of ends and principles. The real arena is corrupt and bloody. Life is a corrupting process . . . he who fears corruption fears life."[6] These are comforting words to anyone who needs to break the rules and is looking to justify their crimes as serving a higher good. Since life is corrupt, according to Alinsky, everyone is corrupt, and corruption is just business as usual. "In action," Alinsky writes, "one does not always enjoy the luxury of a decision that is consistent both with one's individual conscience and the good of mankind. The choice must always be for the latter."[7] But who is to determine what is good for mankind—the progressive elite? Alinsky's creed is a creed that will justify anything.

Practicing deception to conceal one's true goals and regarding moral principles and laws as applicable to others but not to oneself are the core concepts of Alinsky's *Rules for Radicals*. But the all-consuming focus of Alinsky's manual—its strategic end, which these are mere means to achieve—is *power*. The following anecdote about Alinsky's teachings nicely illustrates the focus of Alinsky radicalism: "When Alinsky would ask new students why they wanted to organize, they would invariably respond with selfless bromides about wanting to help others. Alinsky would then scream back at them that there was a one-word answer: 'You want to organize for power!' In *Rules for Radicals*, Alinsky wrote: 'From the moment an organizer enters a community, he lives, dreams, eats, breathes, sleeps only one thing, and that is to build the mass power base of what he calls the army.' "[8]

The New Republic reporter Ryan Lizza interviewed Gregory Galluzzo, one of Barack Obama's three mentors at the Alinsky institute. Galluzzo showed him the training manual they used to teach the future president: "It is filled with workshops and chapter headings on understanding power: 'power analysis,' 'elements of a power organization,' 'the path to power.' Galluzzo told me that many new trainees have an aversion to Alinsky's gritty approach because they come to organizing as idealists rather than realists. The Alinsky manual instructs them to get over these hang-ups. 'We are not virtuous by not wanting power,' it says. 'We are really cowards for not wanting power,' because 'power is good' and 'powerlessness is evil.'"[9] For Alinsky and his followers, power—a means—is in fact the end.

The quest for power in the belief that acquiring it can be world-transforming is the key to understanding the motivations and methods of today's progressives, like Hillary Clinton. In March 2007, the *Washington Post* reported that Hillary Clinton had kept her ties to the Alinsky movement even in the White House, from which she gave support to Alinsky's organization and its radical agendas.[10]

The quest for power as the first priority, the need to conceal one's true agenda, and the assurance that the rules don't apply to radicals who break them in service to the cause make up the core message of Alinsky's teaching. These are the political guidelines for modern progressives and the Democratic Party today.

PART II

THE AGENDA

1

Obamacare

An Attack on Individual Freedom

During the protests of the sixties, activists on the left used to tell each other, "The issue is never the issue; the issue is always the revolution." "Issues" are viewed as instrumental—means of accumulating the support and power that will make it possible to fundamentally change the social order. The slogans and proposals that radicals believe are necessary to advance their agendas will not always seem radical. Alinsky put it this way: "Any revolutionary change must be preceded by a passive, affirmative, non-challenging attitude toward change among the mass of our people."[1] In other words, it is first necessary to sell the people on change itself, the "audacity of hope," and "yes we can." Then one proceeds by proposing moderate changes that open the door to more radical solutions. Alinsky said, "Remember: once you organize people around something as commonly agreed upon as pollution, then an organized people is on the move. From there it's a short and natural step to political pollution, to Pentagon pollution."[2]

Today, Alinsky progressives—first and foremost Obama and Clinton—are leaders of the Democratic Party, which they have transformed from a party of the liberal center into a party of the political left. Clinton's running mate, Tim Kaine, is a former Christic Institute Marxist who supported the communist guerrillas in Central America during the Cold War. Bernie Sanders, whose constituency is a vital wing of the Democratic Party, is a lifelong supporter of communist causes, despite his campaign claim that the socialism he aspires to is Denmark's. These standout figures are just reflections of the fact that the Democratic Party has moved so far to the left in recent decades that it now operates on the sixties' principle that the issues it advances are mere stepping stones on the way to more radical changes.

Nowhere is this principle more clearly visible than in the design and passage of the Affordable Care Act, or Obamacare, the signature legislation of the Obama administration, and reincarnation of the socialized health care program that Hillary Clinton attempted to pass more than 20 years earlier. Before it even came to a vote, public opinion polls showed that a majority of Americans rejected the plan. But despite the controversial nature and society-wide implications of the 2,700-page bill that no legislator even claimed to have read, the Democrats used their congressional majorities to ram Obamacare into law without a single Republican vote. This was unprecedented for such comprehensive society-affecting legislation. Social Security and Medicare, its predecessors, were passed with overwhelming majorities in both political parties. Their legislative sponsors understood that if such all-encompassing legislation were to be imposed by a partisan majority, it would sow deep divisions in the nation and unsettle the social contract.

When Obamacare was proposed, it was already so radical that securing a majority of Republican votes was impossible. Nonetheless, there were perhaps a dozen Republicans in Congress who expressed a willingness to support it, among them Senators Susan Collins and Olympia Snowe. But the Democrats were unwilling to make any concessions even to moderate Republican concerns because they regarded Obamacare as epoch-making legislation, a crucial building block of the progressive future; and they were prepared to use their congressional monopoly and disregard other considerations to put the cornerstone in place.

This radical legislation was so important to Democrats that the new president spent the lion's share of his political capital during his first year in office on the effort to pass the bill. With the Democrats solidly behind him, Obama made the Affordable Care Act his focus even though the nation was in the throes of its worst economic crisis since the Great Depression. Instead of concentrating on jobs and the economy, Obama and the Democrats spent the first 15 months of the new administration pushing a massive and costly new health care program. If Obama and the Democrats were concerned about dealing with the jobs crisis, they would not have used their monopoly power to pursue a new trillion-dollar social program opposed by more than half the nation and by every Republican in Congress. But they were not as interested in addressing the crisis, let alone uniting the country, as they were in using the new legislation as leverage to launch their society-transforming schemes.

Because Obamacare represented a radical departure, a stepping stone to socialized medicine already rejected by Americans during the Clinton administration, Democrats had to resort to deception to pass it, even with their bicameral majorities. To sell Obamacare to the American public, the president employed several blatantly false claims, which he repeated over and over, most notoriously: "If you like your health care plan, you can keep it." This particular falsehood was named "Lie of the Year" by the Pulitzer Prize–winning (and left-leaning) website Politifact.com.[3] Obama also told the public, "You can keep your doctor if you like him," another lie. He also lied in assuring taxpayers footing the bill that it was not a tax and that its benefits would not be available to people who entered the country illegally. This assertion was part of his State of the Union message, which provoked Representative Joe Wilson to shout, "You lie," causing a blizzard of criticism to descend on him for an outburst that was deemed a rude and inappropriate offense to both the president and the Congress, even though it was true.[4]

The Obamacare lies were not incidental; they were instrumental. They were required because the real plan for Obamacare violated several core American principles that could only be overcome by stealth. America's constitutional framework is based on individual rights and individual freedoms. Until the passage of Obamacare, the right of

Americans to choose their doctor—someone to guide them through life-and-death decisions—was part of the American social contract. The same was true of the right to choose one's health care plan. Obama and the Democrats were able to subvert both these individual freedoms only because they deliberately pretended Obamacare wouldn't do just that. The same was true of the provision that provided health benefits to illegal aliens—including taxpayer subsidies if they couldn't afford the care. Providing illegal aliens with subsidies and medical benefits is, of course, a powerful magnet for more illegal immigration. It is also an assault on the idea of citizenship as the foundation for the constitutional rights afforded specifically to Americans who, over the generations, fought to create and defend them and gave their lives to do so.

The lies were even used to deceive the Congressional Budget Office and the Democrats in Congress who passed it. In an unguarded videotaped moment during a panel discussion at the University of Pennsylvania, Jonathan Gruber, a principal architect of the plan, revealed the reasoning behind the lies: "This bill was written in a tortured way to make sure [the Congressional Budget Office] did not score the mandate as taxes. If CBO scored the mandate as taxes, the bill dies, okay? . . . If you made it explicit that healthy people pay in and sick people get money, it would not have passed, okay? Lack of transparency is a huge political advantage. And basically, you know, call it the stupidity of the American voter or whatever. But basically that was really, really critical to getting the thing to pass."[5]

This is a revealing confession on several counts. First, Obamacare was a plan to redistribute wealth by transferring income from young people to old and through subsidies to those who could not afford it paid by those who could. But the Democrats recognized that even with a two-house majority and a monopoly of government power, they could not run such a socialist scheme past the American people. Not if they were truthful and made an honest appeal to American voters. *Lack of transparency is a huge political advantage.* Gruber, who was paid more than half a million dollars for his services and deceptions, is an MIT liberal. But this statement could have been made by any common despot. And it is this brand of despotism that characterizes the entire campaign to enact the primary legislative achievement of the Obama era.

In the short span in which it has been implemented, Obamacare has been a catastrophic failure. Insurance premiums and policy deductibles have skyrocketed—despite solemn promises that Obamacare would lower costs—while almost every Obamacare state exchange has gone bankrupt. To address this crisis, Hillary Clinton vowed in her campaign to "defend and expand the Affordable Care Act." To accomplish this, she vowed to implement a "public option," which is another name for a so-called single-payer plan, where the "single payer" is the US government.[6]

2

The Environment

A Pretext for Government Control

PAUSE FOR A MOMENT over the "public option" and what it means. It means that the government, and more than likely a single government agency, would eventually have access to the health and financial information of every American—all 330 million—and would also control their ability to gain life-extending drugs and medical treatments should they need them. "Death panels" are an inevitable element of any government health care monopoly, which inevitably requires a rationing of services. It means that unscrupulous government bureaucrats would have vital information about any individual to use as blackmail against political opponents. This is the basis not only for a socialist state but for a totalitarian one in which every individual is at the mercy of the rulers.

That a totalitarian infrastructure, in which the life of every individual comes under government scrutiny and control, should be the endpoint of progressive schemes should surprise no one. Ever-expanding control of the individual and "the private sector" is integral to the Democratic Party's agenda to create a progressive future and remold the people who inhabit it. This should be cause for concern for everyone. Progressives are results-oriented and control-driven. Their dedication to social engineering brings with it a disdain for constitutional order and, in particular, for deliberative bodies, like Congress, that reflect the diverse, unruly, and frustrating predilections of the population at large. The constitutional architect James Madison warned of this danger in *Federalist* #47: "The accumulation of all powers, legislative, executive, and judiciary, in the same hands, whether of one, a few, or many, and whether hereditary, self-appointed, or elective, may justly be pronounced the very definition of tyranny."[1]

As two *National Review* writers point out, an especially clear illustration of this threat is the Obama administration's implementation of its environmental agenda, which Clinton promised in her campaign to expand. "Without congressional authorization," write Yuval Levin and Ramesh Ponneru, "the administration has used the Environmental Protection Agency, the supposedly independent Nuclear Regulatory Commission, and other agencies to pressure energy producers, the auto industry, power utilities, and others to toe the president's preferred line. In one particularly egregious instance, the EPA moved in 2014 to require the states to regulate electricity production and consumption to meet a set of arbitrary carbon dioxide-emission targets—under threat of restricting their residents' access to electricity."[2]

The environment provides the perfect pretext for progressives in Washington to expand their control over the lives of Americans, whom they obviously regard as subjects rather than citizens. *And basically, you know, call it the stupidity of the American voter or whatever.*[3] The environmental movement to "save the planet" is a textbook case of the dream of a secular redemption that inspires the left and fuels its appetite for power. If the goal is saving the planet, why allow constitutional obstacles like the separation of powers or the sovereignty of the people or truth to get in the way? While poll after poll shows that climate change ranks way down on the list of Americans' concerns, progressive elites are confident that the public is wrong.

For the true zealots of the environmental left like Bernie Sanders, "climate change" is, in fact, the greatest threat to national security—greater than ISIS or al-Qaeda. Sanders actually made such a statement during the second presidential primary debate. When challenged about the extravagance of the claim, he stood by it: "Absolutely. Climate change is directly related to the growth of terrorism and if we do not get our act together and listen to what the scientists say, you're going to see countries all over the world . . . struggling over limited amounts of water and land to grow their crops and you're going to see all kinds of conflict."[4]

Hillary's view of the environmental challenge was nearly as dire: "Climate change is an urgent threat and a defining challenge of our time. It threatens our economy, our national security, and our children's health and futures."[5] Such an urgency translated into Clinton's opposition to fracking, the Keystone pipeline, and support for her party's general war on fossil fuels—in other words, a continuation of the progressive drive to remake America's energy infrastructure without the consent of the people.

3

The Myth of Systemic Racism

LIKE THE QUEST FOR power, the need for control is driven by the progressive desire for a radical transformation of American society. On the eve of his election in 2008, Barack Obama declared, "We are five days away from fundamentally transforming the United States of America."[1] Fifteen years before that, First Lady Hillary Clinton had offered her vision of the future in a speech in Austin, Texas: "Let us be willing to remold society by redefining what it means to be a human being in the 20th century, moving into a new millennium."[2] Long before her speech, the Soviets had set out to create "a new man and new woman," to people the communist future they were creating. It's an essential element of the progressive vision that everyone becomes politically correct. The 2016

Democratic Party platform states, "We will push for societal transformation," a warning that progressives are serious when it comes to revolutionary change.[3]

Progressives have been working toward this transformation as far back as the administration of Woodrow Wilson, when they moved to centralize power in Washington and create vast new bureaucracies of experts that would exercise "executive, legislative, and judicial powers without the consent of the people or its elected representatives."[4] Prominent among the new bureaucracies now are offices of "diversity," which have assigned American citizens to categories of "disadvantaged," "oppressed," and "underrepresented" groups and provided them with privileges based on race, gender, and ethnicity. This "identity politics" and its goal of "social justice" are radical departures from America's social contract. By empowering groups instead of individuals, they are, in fact, antithetical to the principles of the American founding, which proclaim that individuals–regardless of what groups they belong to–have God-given rights that are inalienable and that government cannot subordinate or take away.

Under the Fourteenth Amendment, all American citizens are guaranteed equal rights under the law. Nonetheless, in the postslavery South, discriminatory laws and practices persisted for nearly a hundred years. This injustice was rectified when discriminatory practices were outlawed by the Civil Rights Act, which ended segregation 50 years ago. The civil rights revolution should have put an end to government-imposed racial categories that privileged some groups over others and deprived individuals of their right to equal treatment under the law. But Democrats have spent the last

50 years reintroducing racial categories into virtually every aspect of public life and creating bureaucracies to enforce race-based privileges for designated groups. Discriminatory policies have also been extended to gender and ethnic groups through "affirmative action" measures justified as remedying past discrimination. Like progressive measures generally, these temporary remedies have proved to be the camel's nose under the tent and are now a permanent structure of the social order and a guiding feature of the Democratic agenda.

While institutional or systemic racism has been illegal in America for 50 years, the 2016 Democratic Party platform promises that "Democrats will fight to end institutional and systemic racism in our society."[5] There is no evidence that such racism actually exists. It is asserted in a sleight of hand that attributes every statistical disparity affecting allegedly "oppressed" groups to prejudice against them because of their identity. This "prejudice," however, is a progressive myth. This is not to say that there aren't individuals who are prejudiced. But there is no systemic racism in America's institutions, and if there is, it is already illegal and easily remedied.

A politically correct term for identifying the results of alleged systemic prejudice is "underrepresentation." For progressives, underrepresentation is proof that there is systemic discrimination. But is it? Ninety percent of the multimillionaires in the National Basketball Association are black. Are whites and Hispanics and Asians systematically discriminated against to keep them out of this lucrative profession? Progressives claim that as a matter of social justice, a place at the table—admissions, jobs—must be found for underrepresented groups. But why are they underrepresented? Has one racist admissions officer been identified in the offices of America's liberal colleges? Is there a single qualified black or Hispanic or Native American individual who has been denied university admission on the basis of their collective group identity? Is there one faculty candidate who has been denied a position because of their gender or race? In the absence of such evidence, a fair-minded observer would conclude that they failed as individuals to meet other—nonracial, nongender—standards. Perhaps their failure is attributable to cultural or economic issues rather than their race or gender. Women actually constitute a majority of college students. How is that possible if there is a gender hierarchy that oppresses them?

If an individual fails to gain a job or admission to an institution, the traditional American way has been to look to the qualifications of the individual to explain the rejection. Or to examine the measures used to screen applicants to see if there are discriminatory double standards. But under the progressive mandate, collective identities trump individual qualifications, and collective privileges replace individual rights. The consequences of this transformation are most visible in the American university, which over the last four decades has become the first major institution to be transformed by progressives. As a consequence, the curriculum has been turned over to "oppression studies," in which white male Americans are the villains. Racial, ethnic, and gender privileges have been reinstituted by college administrators, and collegiate campuses have become the sites of segregated student housing, segregated student associations, "spaces of color" for nonwhites only, and even segregated graduations.

Universities are the training institutions for the nation's future politicians, judges, journalists, and teachers, and therefore engines of the larger social transformation progressives seek. The identity politics and oppression myths of the left are already creating a hierarchy of social privilege in American society, along with increasing social divisions and conflicts. It is no coincidence that the cultural dominance of the left and eight years of the Obama administration have divided the nation along racial lines to a degree not seen for generations. Since membership in a racial, ethnic, or gender group enhances an individual's status and social power, it is also an incentive to emphasize differences and claim more special treatment and exemption from the standards that govern others, hence the increasing Balkanization of the American public.

4

Globalism and Radical Islam

THE IDEA OF *e pluribus unum*—out of many one—was once the cornerstone of the American social contract. What made this contract work was the commitment to a common American culture based on the freedom and equality of *individuals* and the commitment of immigrant groups to assimilate and become Americans. Progressives have declared war on this social contract in favor of a society of government-enforced group identities and racial and gender privileges. The politically correct but factually inaccurate term *undocumented immigrant* is a typical weapon in the war to transform America's society and culture. It is now employed by universities, the media, and the Democratic Party to describe—and exculpate—people who have entered the country illegally.

Those who use it are colluding in the destruction of American sovereignty and citizenship.

The term *undocumented* makes real-world sense only if someone has gone through a legal process and lost their documents, not if they have never had them, not if they have actually broken the law, violating America's borders and circumventing an entry process that would normally include screening for communicable diseases, commitment to democratic order, and readiness to defend the nation and contribute to its prosperity. Absent this process, *invasion* is the accurate term to describe what 11 million illegal aliens have done with the encouragement and support of the Democratic Party. Insistence on the term *undocumented* as a replacement for "illegal" signifies that America's laws deserve no respect and that American citizenship as a set of commitments and obligations (and not merely rights and privileges) is meaningless. Obama's unconstitutional executive amnesty for those here illegally put the American presidency solidly behind this anti-American agenda, and the Democratic Party to a man is behind him. The erasure of the American republic is the core agenda of the Democratic Party.

Assimilation into America's culture and allegiance to its constitutional framework were once obligations of immigrants coming to these shores. No longer. As Hudson fellow John Fonte observes, "In the past, American presidents emphasized the life-altering change that occurs when an immigrant renounces prior political loyalties to take the Oath of Allegiance to the United States, leaving one people to join another. By contrast, President Obama, in a promotional video, says becoming an American citizen is 'not about changing who you are; it's about adding a new chapter on your journey.'"[1] In accordance with this revisionist view, in 2015 Obama watered down the Oath of Allegiance to allow immigrants who were conscientious objectors, or perhaps adherents to the Islamic holy war against the United States, to ignore the pledge "to bear arms on behalf of the United States."[2]

Donald Trump was right to emphasize the border crisis and the problem of illegal immigration in his presidential campaign. He was right to declare that "we don't have a country without a border."[3] By contrast, Clinton promised during the campaign to follow and extend Obama's immigration policies, including his offer of amnesty, and to create a path to citizenship rights and privileges for millions of people who are in the country illegally. In a private speech to Brazilian bankers in May 2013, Clinton revealed that her "dream" was to have "open borders" for the 600 million inhabitants of the western hemisphere.[4] This progressive fantasy discounts the achievements that created America's unique success and therefore ignores the vast *cultural* differences that have made resource-rich countries like Mexico poor and resource-poor countries like Japan prosperous. It is America's unique culture that has made the nation prosperous and great, and it is on this culture that progressives have declared war. The dream of open borders captures the contempt with which progressives regard America's sovereignty and the hard-won achievements of its people. Democratic immigration policy undermines the values that made these achievements possible and is an attempt to redefine what it actually means to be an American.

The lynchpin of this redefinition is the replacement of *assimilation* as a goal with *integration*—a concept designed to emphasize the preservation of the cultural and linguistic differences of immigrants' origins. "Integration" is the politically correct way of emphasizing, in Obama's words, that immigration is "not about changing who you are; it's about adding a new chapter on your journey." The emphasis on the diversity of identities and cultures is structured to fit the left's oppression paradigm. In the words of John Fonte, "The new, transformed civic morality of the progressive narrative . . . divides Americans between dominant or 'oppressor' groups—whites, males, native-born, Christians, heterosexuals—and victim or 'oppressed' groups—racial, ethnic, and linguistic minorities; women; LGBT individuals, and 'undocumented' immigrants. Progressive politics doesn't seek the national interest or the common good. Its purpose is to promote 'marginalized' or 'oppressed' groups against 'dominant' or 'oppressor' groups."[5] It is the old Marxist wine in new bottles, and the results are bound to be similar.

Progressives have devised a politically correct term—*people of color*—to enforce their oppression worldview. "People of color" is not even grammatical English but a French construction. Its purpose is to create a vast new alleged victim group and further isolate the white European American majority as an oppressor of everyone else. The effect of employing the term *people of color* is to erase the distinction, for example, between the descendants of Spanish conquistadors who ravaged the indigenous Indians of Mexico and the Indians they conquered and killed. They are both now "people of color" and therefore oppressed, deserving of special sympathy and privilege as a matter of "social justice." Virtually all the immigrants and refugees for whom the Democrats seek amnesty and asylum belong to the ideological category "people of color" and are therefore viewed by progressives as minorities and victims—and potential recruits for the Democratic Party.

A particularly aggressive instance of the left's anti-American agenda, related to immigration, is the establishment of "Sanctuary Cities," which are supported by the entire Democratic Party. Sanctuary Cities are so described because their officials are pledged to defy immigration law and offer a safe haven to people who have entered the United States illegally, including serial felons who have already wreaked havoc on hundreds of thousands of innocent Americans. Sanctuary Cities were created by leftists immediately following the terrorist attacks on 9/11 as an explicit effort to counter the attempts of the newly created Department of Homeland Security to protect Americans from further assaults. Sanctuary Cities have been established in 340 Democrat-controlled municipalities across the United States through resolutions that pledge noncooperation with the Department of Homeland Security and its immigration officers.

Behind the movement to create Sanctuary Cities were two radical organizations—the American Civil Liberties Union and the Center for Constitutional Rights. Both organizations opposed the Patriot Act and the war in Afghanistan to bring the perpetrators of 9/11 to justice. Both provided political and legal support to domestic enemies like Sami al-Arian, a leader of Palestine Islamic Jihad eventually deported for his terrorist activities, and for the prisoners at Guantanamo Bay captured on the battlefield in Afghanistan.[6] The resolutions—really acts of sedition—were passed by their Democratic allies, turning them into Sanctuary Cities:

> Therefore, be it resolved that the council of the city of______...
>
> Directs the Police Department of the City of_________ to:
>
> (a) refrain from participating in the enforcement of federal immigration laws;
>
> (b) seek adequate written assurances from federal authorities that residents of the City of_____ who are placed in federal custody will not be subjected to military detention; secret detention; secret immigration proceedings; or detention without access to counsel, and refrain from assisting federal authorities to obtain custody of such individuals absent such assurances.
>
> (c) refrain, whether acting alone or with federal or state law enforcement officers, from collecting or maintaining information about the political, religious or social views, associations or activities of any individual, group, association, organization, corporation, business or partnership unless such information directly relates to an investigation of criminal activities, and there are reasonable grounds to suspect the subject of the information is or may be involved in criminal conduct;
>
> (d) refrain from the practice of stopping drivers or pedestrians for the purpose of scrutinizing their identification documents without particularized suspicion of criminal activity...[7]

A crucial element of this effort to obstruct America's war on Islamic terrorists was point c, the injunction against obtaining information about the religious views or associations of individuals until after they had actually committed a crime, which in the case of Islamic radicals could mean scores or thousands of victims. America is the target of a religious war. Consequently, such a ban places serious obstacles in the way of officials attempting to assess threats and prevent them before they happen. The Boston Marathon bombers, the San Bernardino and Orlando killers—all Islamic jihadists—were on the FBI's radar before their attacks but slipped off because of the prohibitions against taking their religious commitments and associations into account.

This denial about the nature of America's enemy is pervasive among America's intelligence services and first-responder offices thanks to the determined efforts by the Democratic Party, particularly since Obama's election in 2008. Before this political correctness set in, the 9/11 Commission Report on the Islamic attacks of September 2001 referred to "Islam" 322 times, used the word "Muslim" 145 times, and used "jihad" (holy war) 126 times. But according to Republican congressman Louie Gohmert, "The current FBI counterterrorism lexicon, which describes the language [agents] can use, does not include 'jihad,' and does not include 'Muslim,' does not include 'Islam.' It includes 'violent extremism' many times, but it does not include 'sharia' [the Islamic law jihadists are seeking to impose globally]. It does not even include 'Al-Qaeda,' 'Hezbollah,' or 'Hamas.' Even the National Intelligence Strategy 2009 does not include references to '*jihad*,' 'Muslim,' or 'Islam,'" while the Obama administration officially describes the war Islamic radicals have declared on the United States as "overseas contingency operations."[8]

The Democratic Party has never been comfortable with the war against radical Islam or willing to acknowledge its religious nature. After the first bombing of the World Trade Center in 1993 when six Americans were killed and a thousand injured, President Bill Clinton did not even visit the site and attempted to treat it as an isolated attack by individual criminals. This denial persisted through several major terrorist attacks on US assets and despite Osama bin Laden's 1996 "Declaration of War against the Americans Occupying the Land of the Two Holy Places."[9] It made Democrats reluctant partners in the war in Iraq, early opponents of the Guantanamo holding facility and military tribunals, and proponents of prosecuting the mastermind of 9/11 and other Islamic terrorists in civilian courts.

This discomfort flows from the progressive view that Islam is a religion of "people of color" and therefore oppressed. Consequently, Muslims require special protections and allowances that might seem imprudent from a security point of view. Surveys by Al-Jazeera and other groups show that hundreds of millions of Muslims hold radical beliefs, including support for the holy war against "infidels."[10] Democrats oppose the surveillance of mosques, which are mainly financed by Saudi Arabia, a fundamentalist Islamic state, and are centers of recruitment to jihadist agendas. Democrats were appalled when Donald Trump proposed a temporary moratorium on Muslim immigration until proper vetting procedures were instituted. Trump's concern with the vetting problems for a religious group whose beliefs were at odds with the American Constitution and millions of whose members supported a holy war against the United States was denounced as bigotry by progressives.

While hundreds of millions of individual Muslims are law-abiding and peaceful, Islam itself—far from being a religion of the oppressed—is a religion of domination and submission. The Arabic word *Islam* means "submission," and the Koran clearly enjoins its followers to treat other religions as requiring just that. Theocratic Islam is not only a religion but also a political ideology recognizing no separation between mosque and state. Submission to its religious law—sharia—is thus to be enforced by the state. Unlike Christianity or Judaism, Islam is a supremacist religion that regards non-Muslims as infidels who must be eliminated or subdued. In words that are holy writ today, its Prophet incites believers to behead unbelievers and pursue a war of terror against them: "I am with you, therefore make firm those who believe. I will cast terror into the hearts of those who disbelieve. Therefore strike off their heads and strike off every fingertip of them."[11] To regard ISIS and al-Qaeda as a perversion of the religion rather than a radical interpretation of its texts—as Democrats do—is denial and is dangerous.

The effects of these beliefs are etched in Islam's 1,400-year history of bloody conquest, including a modern genocide in Armenia and contemporary genocides against Christians and Yazidis in Syria and Iraq. Sponsors of Islamic terrorism like the Muslim Brotherhood and powerful Islamic states, most notably Iran, are promoting a genocidal war against the Jews and openly seek to establish a global caliphate—a world state under Islamic law—that would abrogate all the constitutions that guarantee basic freedoms and individual rights.

Democrats' discomfort with the war against radical Islam—with even calling it a "war against radical Islam"—is also consistent with their discomfort with almost any war that America has found itself in over the last half century. This is attributable to progressives' politically correct prism, through which they see America as a predominantly white, capitalist superpower and therefore in the category of oppressive states. Consequently, progressives regard America generally as a source of international problems rather than of potential solutions. These attitudes have led Democrats to promote a downgrading of American military power and influence, which has emboldened America's adversaries, Russia and China, and resulted in an expansion of their influence in Europe, Asia, and the Middle East.

Democratic policies of appeasement and retreat have led to three disastrous Democratic policy decisions in the war with radical Islam. The first was the bloodless surrendering of Iraq to ISIS and Iran. As commander-in-chief, Obama rejected the counsel of his Joint Chiefs of Staff following America's victory in the Iraq War and made no effort to retain America's giant military base in Iraq's "Green Zone" or to keep a recommended force of up to 20,000 US troops in the country. Such a military presence would have smothered the ISIS terror network in its cradle. Instead, the vacuum created by America's withdrawal led rapidly to the emergence of ISIS as the largest terror organization in history, with tentacles in Iraq, Syria, Yemen, North Africa, and other countries around the world. It also led to the slaughter of hundreds of thousands of Christians, Yazidis, and other "infidels" and chaos throughout the Fertile Crescent that created 20 million refugees across the region while Obama was in office.

Second, Obama's Middle Eastern retreat was crystallized by his failure to enforce the "red line" he had drawn in Syria to prevent its dictator from using chemical weapons. This capitulation allowed Russia to move into the region, replacing America as its dominant external power. Third, at the same time, Obama directed harsh diplomatic moves against Israel's leader, Benjamin Netanyahu, and Egypt's Hosni Mubarak, another American ally. In the midst of public demonstrations against the Egyptian regime, he declared that Mubarak must step down, effectively driving Mubarak out of power while giving political support to the Muslim Brotherhood to replace him.[12] This reprised Jimmy Carter's attack on the Shah of Iran, an American ally, which led directly to the creation of the first Islamic terrorist state. The fall of Mubarak paved the way for the ascension of the previously outlawed Muslim Brotherhood, the organization that had nurtured Osama bin Laden and provided the ideological foundations for the Islamic holy war. When the Egyptian military toppled the Brotherhood, the White House cut off military aid to the new regime, driving the largest Arab nation into the arms of the Russians.

The Democrats' appeasement of America's enemies and betrayal of America's allies achieved an apotheosis in a nuclear deal with Iran, a nation that has been at war with America and the West since 1979. Iran is the chief sponsor of international terror and directly responsible for thousands of American deaths, beginning with the massacre of 241 US marines in Lebanon in 1983 and including thousands of

Americans maimed or killed by Iranian IEDs in Iraq. Iran's fanatical leaders were regarded as so dangerous that an international sanctions regime was put in place to weaken Iran and prevent it from developing nuclear weapons. Obama made it a centerpiece of his policy to lift those sanctions and bring an unrepentant and unrehabilitated Iran back into the community of nations.

In 2009, the Iranian people poured into the streets of Teheran in a "Green Revolution" to protest the tyranny of its ruling mullahs and possibly overthrow them. Throughout the demonstrations and the repression and murders of protesters that followed, the Obama administration and its secretary of state were silent, a distinct contrast to their attitude toward the demonstrators in Egypt who—with Obama's encouragement—overthrew an American ally. Washington's silence was a product of the administration's already formed plans to lift the sanctions on Iran, bring the pariah state back into the community of nations, provide it with a path to nuclear weapons, and line its pockets with nearly $200 billion in sweeteners for the deal. When the agreement was concluded, Iran emerged from its status as a pariah nation to become the principal power in the Middle East.

The Iran deal provided that Teheran would essentially police itself in the matter of inspections and whether it adhered to the requirements. During the negotiations, America's diplomatic team also turned a blind eye to Iran's development of ballistic missiles, previously banned by the United Nations, and its aggressive moves in Yemen and other areas of the Middle East.

This was, first of all, a betrayal of America's Middle Eastern ally, Israel, at a time when Iranian leaders were openly predicting that tiny nation would be wiped off the map within 25 years. But it was also a betrayal of America, empowering her mortal enemy, allied now with her Russian and Chinese adversaries. To flaunt their contempt for the American president and his globally recognized weakness, the regime's supreme leader led thousands of Iranians in chants of "Death to America" while the negotiations were still in progress. This insult and threat were also met with silence by Obama and his new secretary of state, John Kerry, whose daughter had married into the Iranian hierarchy.

Because the American public was opposed to the Iran deal by a gaping margin of 28 percent, Obama did not present the agreement to Congress for approval as a treaty. This would have required ratification by two-thirds of the US Senate. Instead, he framed it as an "executive agreement," which would not. Before taking the deal to Congress for approval, he brought it to the UN for ratification, one of several efforts by his administration to erode American sovereignty in favor of a global authority.[13]

And it was a particularly unsavory one. The UN is dominated by a bloc of 57 Islamic states and a collection of dictatorships and kleptocracies notorious for passing resolutions to advance the agendas of terrorist organizations like the Palestinian Authority, Hezbollah, and Hamas. According to NGO "UN Watch," in the 10 years since it was set up, the UN Human Rights Council has passed more resolutions condemning Israel for alleged violations than the rest of the world combined.[14] This is hardly surprising, since the UN

Human Rights Council has been composed of such notorious human rights violators and Jew-hating regimes as Gaddafi's Libya, Communist Cuba, and Iran itself. Yet the UN is a go-to world body for Democratic Party progressives, egged on by their one-world delusions.

The Democrats' globalism is not incidental to their agendas but central. It is behind policies ranging from the Obama administration's decision to turn control of Internet domain names to an international bureaucracy that would allow dictatorial regimes to censor their content to the push for porous and eventually open borders.[15] Democratic justices on the Supreme Court, whose responsibility it is to enforce the US Constitution, regularly defer to international legal authorities, most notoriously Justice Ruth Bader Ginsburg, who, when asked for her advice on drawing up a new constitution for Egypt, said, "I would not look to the U.S. Constitution, if I were drafting a constitution in the year 2012. I might look at the constitution of South Africa. That was a deliberate attempt to have a fundamental instrument of government that embraced basic human rights, have an independent judiciary. It really is, I think, a great piece of work that was done."[16]

It was a revealing choice. The South African Constitution reflects the communist outlook of the leaders of the African National Congress who wrote it and provides as much protection for South Africans as the notorious Stalin constitution did for the benighted citizenry of Soviet Russia in the 1930s. Like its Soviet counterpart, the South African Constitution is made up of "paper rights," as James Madison would have dismissed them. These are rights that either cannot be enforced or can easily be withdrawn. For example, the South African Constitution includes "the right to be protected against violence." Despite this guarantee, South Africa has a murder rate seven times that of the United States and is the rape capital of the world. The South African Constitution also provides citizens with the right not to be discriminated against on the basis of race or sex—unless the government decides such discrimination is fair. Lest anyone think this is an exaggeration, here is the text itself: "Discrimination on one or more of the grounds listed in subsection (3) is unfair unless it is established that the discrimination is fair."[17]

The South African Constitution is a bill of entitlements—promises by government that government can renege on. This is the very opposite of the rights guaranteed by the US Constitution. The rights guaranteed by the US Constitution are not entitlements but *limits* to governmental power. It is these limits that guarantee individual liberty.

Why do Democrats denigrate the Constitution almost instinctively and regularly circumvent its provisions? Why, for example, has Obama disregarded the Constitution's separation of powers and issued executive orders that usurp the legislative powers of Congress over immigration policy and American sovereignty? Why do Democratic Supreme Court justices invent nonexistent constitutional rights, as in *Roe v. Wade*, to usurp the power of state legislatures to determine policy on abortion? Why do Democratic Supreme Court justices like Ruth Bader Ginsburg openly express their contempt for the Constitution as old and outdated? Why do they want to regard its text as mere prologue and displace it with a "living constitution," which can be changed to accommodate "modern" opinions? Why do they make these changes through the bad faith of unelected justices and not through the amendment process that the Constitution provides?

The answer lies in their impatience to fundamentally transform America to conform to their progressive vision and their conviction that the Constitution's system of checks and balances is a giant obstacle in their way. And they are right about that. As Madison explained in *Federalist* #10, the checks and balances of the Constitution were designed to prevent a tyranny of the majority and to "thwart" radical schemes to redistribute income, which he described as "a rage for paper money, for an abolition of debts, for an equal division of property, or for any other improper or wicked project."[18] Understanding that the chief architect of the Constitution regarded progressive agendas like redistribution as "wicked" and that the Constitution was designed to frustrate their designs helps focus progressives on the fact that the Constitution is a barrier to the future they desire. This, in turn, explains why they are so determined to find ways to circumvent or alter it through the power of the justices to invent new rights, as in *Roe v. Wade*, and to reinterpret the document itself as a "living constitution" that exists to accommodate their political and social prejudices.

In the third presidential debate, Hillary Clinton was asked about her attitude toward the Constitution and specifically according to what principles she thought it should be interpreted. Her answer was not an answer to the actual question but was revealing nonetheless: "The Supreme Court should represent all of us. That's how I see the Court. And the kind of people that I would be looking to nominate to the court would be in the great tradition of standing up to the powerful, standing up on our behalf of our rights as Americans."[19] In other words, Clinton, like other proponents of a "living Constitution," sees the court not as a guardian of the principles on which the nation was founded and not as a document designed to limit governmental power. Instead, she sees it as a political instrument for carrying out the will of a political majority—exactly what the framers were determined to prevent.

Regarding the Supreme Court as an institution that should represent the will of the people, let alone that it should be a weapon in a class war against the successful and powerful, is not a constitutional view of its function. It is the opposite. It is an anticonstitutional view that, if it were to prevail, would destroy the framework the founders created and that has served the nation so well. In the constitutional scheme, it is the House of Representatives that is the governmental body designed to represent the people, which is why its members are elected every two years, while Supreme Court justices are appointed for life. It is a very dangerous view that holds that the Supreme Court should represent the people against those whom Clinton regards as powerful (apparently not herself). Such a court could hardly enforce the fundamental principle of American democracy that everyone is equal before the law.

The one specific Supreme Court decision mentioned by Clinton in the presidential debates, along with her determination to see it reversed, was *Citizens United v. Federal Election Commission*. In that case, a 5–4 majority pitting court conservatives against court liberals held that the government could not prevent independent political expenditures by a nonprofit corporation. To do so would be an unacceptable limit on free speech. "If the First Amendment has any force," Justice Kennedy wrote for the majority, "it prohibits Congress from fining or jailing citizens, or associations of citizens, for simply engaging in political speech."[20]

During her campaign, Clinton vowed to introduce a constitutional amendment within her first 30 days in office to overturn the *Citizens United* decision. In a statement, one of her spokesman explained: "The amendment would allow Americans to establish common sense rules to protect against the undue influence of billionaires and special interests and to restore the role of average voters in elections."[21] The spokesman did not explain why Hillary's huge fees to give closed speeches at Wall Street firms and make private commitments to banks like Goldman Sachs would not represent an undue influence of billionaires and special interests, whereas forming voluntary associations to openly express political opinions would.

Opposition to *Citizens United* is but one front in a general war Democrats are conducting on free speech and the First Amendment.[22] This war includes the violent attacks on Trump campaign events during the 2016 election, directed from the DNC and the Obama White House. It includes the drive of universities—a political base of the Democratic Party—to purge Republicans and conservatives from their faculties. A recent study headed by sociologist Daniel Klein recently found that in 1,500 American universities, the ratio of Democrat-voting members to Republican-voting members in history departments was 33.5–1. In journalism and communications departments, the ratio was 20–1.[23] The war against the First Amendment also includes universities' drives to ban "hate speech"—a vague term that more often than not includes conservative dissent from progressive orthodoxies—and to make their campuses "safe places" for left-wing ideas.

As part of her presidential campaign, Clinton proposed a $500 million investment in "antibullying" programs for schools. She immediately tied her proposal to her opponent's political rhetoric in a campaign ad, in which she said, "I don't want bullies in my life, and I especially don't one in the White House."[24] But bullying speech is in the eye of the beholder and is constitutionally protected precisely because the unscrupulous can misrepresent words they disagree with as words that offend them. The political left has already developed an elaborate theory of "microaggressions" to label perceived verbal disrespect for so-called marginal or oppressed groups as being beyond the pale. According to Wikipedia's page on microaggressions, they have "also been defined as 'rooted in racism, sexism, or discrimination based on nationality or sexual orientation. [They] can be delivered casually or even unconsciously.' "[25] Unconsciously! In other words, it is a category invented by the politically correct to stigmatize those who are not.

How far can this assault on speech be taken? In June 2015, Obama's former Department of Homeland Security chief, Janet Napolitano, now president of the University of California, issued an order to her faculty warning them not to utter the following statements that she deemed unacceptable microaggressions: "America is the land of opportunity," "There is only one race, the human race," "I believe the most qualified person should get the job," "Everyone can succeed in this country, if they work hard enough," and "When I look at you, I don't see color."[26]

Obviously this is not just an assault on free speech. It is an assault on America and on everyone consigned to an "oppressor" group, particularly if they do *not* have negative feelings toward "people of color." Otherwise, why proscribe the statement "When I look at you, I don't see color"? The same penchant for suppressing politically incorrect ideas was manifest in Clinton's support for a UN resolution designed by the Islamic bloc to criminalize critics of Islam as "Islamophobic."[27] The term *Islamophobia* was originally coined by the Muslim Brotherhood to silence critics of Islamic terrorism and misogyny. Alleged "Islamophobia" is also an important concern of such key Democratic institutions as the Center for American Progress, a 501c3 financed by the Clintons and George Soros. Until he was hired as Clinton's presidential campaign manager, the center was run by John Podesta. Under Podesta's leadership, it published a $100,000 "report" called *Fear, Inc.*, which stigmatized every major critic of Islamic terrorism and misogyny as an Islamophobe.[28]

With the proper government enforcement, this is how a totalitarian future looks. Ideas that challenge the reigning orthodoxy are identified as beyond the pale and therefore illegitimate, a form of "hate speech" that needs to be suppressed. It is a logical extension of the progressive view in which political opponents are deposited—and discarded—into a basket of deplorables: racists, sexists, homophobes, Islamophobes, and xenophobes.

PART III

THE STRATEGY

1

The Goal and the Path

THE GOAL IS TO put Democrats on the defensive. This can only be accomplished by taking away their moral high ground—their claim to represent the so-called 99 percent against the 1 percent. The strategy is to expose their hypocrisy and turn their firepower against them—to focus on the races, genders, ethnicities, and classes who suffer because of their policies and under their rule. The strategy is to go for the jugular.

2

It's Time to Take the Gloves Off

THE PROGRESSIVE VISION OF American society as a hierarchy of races, genders, and classes is delusional and destructive, but it has been the dominant force in America's political culture for more than half a century. It is the creed of America's society-shaping institutions—schools and the media—and its party line of political correctness is now the conventional wisdom in America's boardrooms and courts. How can conservatives and Republicans hope to resist the societal transformation Democrats are bent on achieving? How can they stop a movement that is antidemocratic and socialist and determined to weaken America even further in the face of grave threats from powers in Europe, Asia, and the Middle East?

Resistance begins with the will to confront the adversary head on. That is the attitude that characterized Donald Trump's campaign from its inception. But for many conservatives, no-holds-barred, in-your-face brawling is problematic to begin with. Unlike progressives, conservatives are constrained by temperament and precept from engaging in politics as a form of warfare—even though their progressive opponents do so as a matter of course. Conservatives are also realists about human nature and are therefore prone to resignation. Reluctance to go for the jugular and willingness to accept defeat can become a self-fulfilling prophecy. If you are reluctant to fight, you are inevitably headed toward defeat when the other side is relentless and despises you. It is only for those who persist in the battle and never let up that the possibility of changing the result comes into view.

In thinking about how progressives approach these battles, consider Bernie Sanders, who has spent a lifetime on the left supporting the communist cause. In 1989, communism collapsed amid a sea of human corpses and economic misery. In other words, it was a catastrophic failure, shattering every dream progressives like Bernie and his comrades ever had. Normal people would have accepted the result and given up the fight for a socialist future. But not Bernie and his comrades. They didn't accept the result, and they didn't give up the fight. They kept on going. They kept up their attacks on America's institutions and renewed their opposition to America's wars. They still believed in the socialist future and the evil 1 percent who exploited everyone else, and they were still ready to fight for what they believed in.

Gradually, their ranks were joined by new generations who were innocent of the tragedies communism had inflicted. Eventually, circumstances changed enough that Bernie was able to run for president as an avowed socialist and win enough support in the Democratic primaries to have captured the nomination if the Clinton cartel hadn't rigged the result.

Republicans have an immediate advantage over Bernie and his progressives. They don't have to live down a monstrous legacy of oppression and failure. But they do have to overcome the habits of complacency and denial that have handcuffed them in the political wars. They have to fight—and fight hard—if they want to defeat the progressive juggernaut that has rolled over them until now.

Before Trump's entry into the presidential primaries, there was not a single Republican figure with a national platform who would have called Hillary Clinton a crook or a liar to her face, although she is both. Before the advent of Trump, there is not a single Republican with a national platform who would have dared to be so politically incorrect. The reason for this is that Republicans are well aware of what happens to anyone who would do so. To be politically *in*correct, one has to believe passionately in one's cause in order to advance it. One has to take the hits and carry on.

In the recent campaign, progressives—always ready to defenestrate an opponent—showed how bloody-minded they can be when the stakes are high enough. The progressive attackers were not merely Democratic Party operatives who have made the politics of personal destruction—character assassination—into an art form. Ludicrous comparisons to

Hitler and Mussolini and fabricated linkages to the Ku Klux Klan were also daily fare in the national media and were even echoed by unhinged "Never Trump" Republicans. Unprincipled and vicious liberal editors were suddenly willing to run unchecked stories with unfounded accusations by women who claimed they had been inappropriately kissed by the candidate 10 and 20 years in the past.[1] In any other context, the same editors would have been fired by their own organizations for such journalistic malfeasance; but in this case, the example was set by the editors of the once august *New York Times*. In a gesture that crystalized this disgraceful performance, the giant Internet site *Huffington Post* appended the following fact-challenged warning to every single news story it ran about Donald Trump: "Editor's note: Donald Trump regularly incites political violence and is a serial liar, rampant xenophobe, racist, misogynist and birther who has repeatedly pledged to ban all Muslims—1.6 billion members of an entire religion—from entering the U.S."[2]

To go on the attack against Democrats when the mainstream media are ready to portray them as champions of minorities, women, and the poor is not for the faint of heart. If they attack you as a racist or call you an obstructionist and you are not prepared to throw those charges back in their faces, you are already losing the war. If your first response is to defend yourself by denying the charge, you are losing the war. To have a chance of winning, your first response must be to attack them in a way that is equally strong, that throws them off balance and puts *them* on the defensive. Mike Tyson summed up this strategy with the following observation: "Everybody has a game plan until you punch them in the mouth." To turn around the political battles conservatives have been losing for so long, they must begin every confrontation by punching progressives in the mouth. To do so, conservatives must develop an attack that takes away progressives' moral superiority and smugness.

3

The Achilles' Heel of the Democratic Party

PROGRESSIVES ARE WILLING TO lie, defame, and destroy for their cause because they are imbued with the idea that what they are doing is noble. They see themselves as the champions of the powerless, voices of the voiceless, and defenders of the underrepresented, the downtrodden, and the "people of color" who are everywhere oppressed. They are intoxicated with their own virtue, which is why no crime they commit or deception they practice can shame them or cause them to break with their own ranks. That is why, with the late and isolated exception of one political consultant, no Democrat defected over Clinton's multiple violations of the Espionage Act, or the multiple corruptions of the Clinton foundation, or the pathological lies of Clinton and her aides to conceal their criminal activities. Not one of them said, "This is a bridge too far. I cannot support her; my party and country deserve better." What justifies for them the actions and lies that to others seem indefensible is the mission, which is to be advanced at all costs. That mission is to beat the deplorables, the irredeemables—the racists, sexists, Islamophobes, et al.—and advance the progressive cause. The only way to bring Democrats down to earth, where they might feel subject to the same standards as everyone else, is to attack them with the same moral force they use to prosecute their mission; the only way to do it is to turn their fire on *them*.

To do this, Republicans need to direct their arrows at the Achilles' heel of the Democratic Party: its monopoly control of the inner cities of America and its responsibility for the misery and suffering inside them. This control stretches over a period of 50 to 100 years in major cities like Chicago, Detroit, Philadelphia, Baltimore, St. Louis, Washington, DC, and many others. These are the centers of America's worst poverty, highest crime rates, failing schools, and general hopelessness. They have been in the hands of Democrats and under their rule for as long as most of the people who inhabit them have been alive. Everything that is wrong with the inner cities of America that policy can affect, Democrats are responsible for: every killing field; every school that year in and year out fails to teach its children the basic skills they need to get ahead; every school that fails to graduate 30 to 40 percent of its charges while those who do get degrees are often functionally illiterate; every welfare system that promotes dependency, condemning its recipients to lifetimes of destitution; every gun-control law that disarms law-abiding citizens in high-crime areas and leaves them defenseless against predators; every catch-and-release policy that puts violent criminals back on the streets; every regulation that ties the hands of police; every material and moral support provided to antipolice agitators like Black Lives Matter, who incite violence against the only protection inner-city families have; every onerous regulation and corporate tax that drives businesses and jobs out of inner-city neighborhoods; every rhetorical assault that tars Democrats' opponents as "racists" and "race traitors," perpetuating a one-party system that denies inner-city inhabitants the leverage and influence of a two-party system. Democrats are responsible for every one of the shackles on inner-city communities, and they have been for 50 to 100 years.

What have Republicans done to oppose *this* racism? What have they done to rally the inhabitants of these Democratic ghettoes to vote out their oppressors and turn these disasters around?

In the 2016 presidential election, the most underreported major proposal was Trump's offer of a "New Deal" for African Americans and other inner-city dwellers. Trump's "New Deal" was composed of three promises. First, for "law and order" and therefore for "safe communities"; second, for a $130 billion scholarship program that would provide inner-city kids with quality educations; and third, for high-paying jobs, which a safe environment and good education would go a long way toward making possible.[1] Trump's vouchers were designed to provide each inner-city child with a tuition of $12,000, which is roughly equivalent to the average tuition in tax-payer dollars already available to send children to public schools that don't teach them.[2]

Consider the impact this would have politically. It would dramatize the Democrats' failure to run decent school systems for the urban poor. It would expose the hypocrisy of Democrats' opposition to vouchers for poor minority children while they send their own children to private schools. It would expose the real interests of the Democratic teacher unions that oppose vouchers because they threaten their stranglehold on K–12 education. If inner-city parents got word that Republicans were offering them $12,000 for each school-age child to secure a decent education, it would blow up the Democratic voting base. Without overwhelming majorities in the urban minority vote, Democrats cannot win national elections. Creating a voucher system that puts the power of the purse in the hands of parents instead of school bureaucrats would break the backs of the teacher unions that provide the biggest slush fund and activist core of the Democratic Party and the greatest opposition to school reform. It would expose the hypocrisy of teacher union officials who send their own children to private schools. It would take away the moral high ground from which Democrats regularly pound their Republican opponents.

The 2016 Democratic Party platform declares, "We will push for a societal transformation to make it clear that black lives matter and that there is no place for racism in our country."[3] If Republicans were to put the racism of the Democrats in the forefront of their speeches and campaigns, it would shred the Democrats' phony but all-too-effective narrative and game plan.

Although Republicans are too polite to mention it, Democrats are the truly racist party. The Civil Rights Act of 1964 outlawed discrimination on the basis of race, religion, color, sex, and national origin and thus outlawed the use of racial categories in hiring and admissions and institutional regulations generally. But Democrats and progressives spent the next 50 years distorting the meaning of the Civil Rights Act and subverting its provisions. As a result, racial categories are now prevalent in virtually every area of American life, spreading injustice and sowing divisions that deepen with every leftist assault on America's color-blind social contract.

This is particularly true of universities, which are the vanguard institutions of the political left and thus foreshadow the American future if the progressive movement should prevail. In American universities today, segregated housing, segregated associations, and even segregated "spaces of color" have become not only accepted but increasingly normal, alongside racially rigged admissions systems that have damaging consequences, including elevated dropout and failure rates for the very minorities they are allegedly designed to help. This is a racism that goes unnamed but could and should be used by conservatives to expose the hypocrisy of people who use race as a political weapon to slander and silence their political opponents.

Until Democratic hypocrisy on race is confronted directly, Republicans will continue to point a loaded gun at their own heads. The 2016 Democratic platform condemns "the racial wealth and income gaps [that] are the result of policies that discriminate against people of color and constrain their ability to earn income and build assets to the same extent as other Americans."[4] There are no such policies, since federal law prohibits discrimination on the basis of race or color. In order to justify this allegation, the Democratic platform claims that "people of color" were "disproportionately targeted for subprime, predatory, and fraudulent mortgages during the run-up to the housing crisis."[5] This is not only false; it turns the facts on their head. The fraudulent mortgages were created by banks held at gunpoint by Bill Clinton, Barney Frank, and Barack Obama, who led a campaign to label bankers as "racist" for rejecting mortgage applications from people who obviously couldn't afford to pay them. Under pressures both legal and extralegal, the bankers caved to the progressives and created loans for people who did not have the means to pay them back. When the house of cards thus built collapsed in the so-called subprime housing crisis, a rash of foreclosures ensued through which the African American middle class lost half of its net worth.[6]

Republicans were well aware of this social disaster and cynical exploitation by its Democratic instigators, but they failed to make this an issue, just as they failed to characterize the economic policies of the Obama years—which took a disproportionate toll on African Americans—as "racist," the way Democrats would have done. The failure to fight battles like this stores up future political defeats, since few people remember what actually happened in the subprime mortgage crisis of 2008, while Democrats are always ready to misrepresent the facts and pin these disasters on their opponents.

The most significant and ominous racial aggression by Democrats is the support they provide to the racist organization Black Lives Matter, which has declared war on police officers across the country and has instigated a series of ambushes and executions of law enforcement officials.[7] These assaults have led to a suspension of the proactive policing procedures that held crime rates in check. A rash of homicides in the wake of the Black Lives Matter protests have cost many hundreds of black lives in cities across America. Since the Ferguson and Freddie Gray riots, an additional 131 homicides have been committed in Baltimore alone, an increase of 70 percent.[8] Black Lives Matter is officially endorsed by the Democratic Party, while Democratic funders like George Soros have raised more than $100 million to empower Black Lives street thugs in the name of "social justice." Directly following the murder of five police officers in Dallas during a Black Lives Matter "protest," President Obama invited its leaders to the White House.

A month before the 2016 elections, 100 Black Lives Matter activists gathered at the University of California to attack the Los Angeles police department with this chant: "LAPD what you say? How many people have you killed today? LAPD you can't hide. We charge you with genocide."[9] The protest was one of hundreds in the last few years attacking police departments for an alleged "genocidal" war against blacks. There is no such war and no factual basis for this charge. A *Wall Street Journal* report shows that police shootings make up 12 percent of all white and Hispanic homicide deaths, which is three times the proportion of black deaths from the same cause. At the same time, according to FBI data, over the last 10 years, 40 percent of cop killers have been black, and police officers are killed by blacks at a rate 2.5 times higher than the rate at which blacks are killed by police.[10]

Black Lives Matter activists and their Democratic allies are practiced liars with statistics. It is true that while blacks make up only 13 percent of the population, they account for 37 percent of the prison population.[11] But blacks commit more than 40 percent of America's violent crimes. The proper baseline for judging whether there is discrimination in overall arrests or shootings is the percentage of black participation in criminal activity, not black representation in the population at large.[12] Nationally, black criminals account for more than 50 percent of the homicides.[13] It stands to reason that they would be involved in a relatively high proportion of the violent encounters between criminals and the police.

Even more preposterous is Black Lives Matter's claim—echoed by many Democrats—that America is a "white supremacist" nation. In addition to being patently absurd, this is itself a racist claim, as it implicates all whites. It is a particular absurdity in 2016, since America—having just elected an African American president twice—is arguably the most tolerant, least racist nation on earth. In the last 16 years, America has had 2 black Secretaries of State, a black Chairman of the Joint Chiefs of Staff, 3 black heads of the National Security Council, and more than 9,000 black elected officials at state and municipal levels.[14] Major American cities like Atlanta, Philadelphia, and Baltimore are run by blacks, and many more are governed by black mayors, black police chiefs, black judges, nonwhite-majority city councils, and black superintendents of schools. How ironic that more than half a century after the end of segregation and the passage of the Civil Rights Act, after the integration of America's military and schools and popular culture, the accusation of "white supremacy"—this racist incitement–should be the emblem of a movement for "social justice."

Yet this is what the Democratic Party believes. Its official platform indicts America as "systemically" racist, and its leader, Barack Obama, has perversely claimed that racism is in America's DNA.[15] There is no way that Republicans can stop the "societal transformation" that Democrats are planning without confronting this mendacity on the race issue. There is no way Republicans can neutralize Democrats' attacks without characterizing Democrats as racists for making this charge, which is a libel against Americans who are white. This may be uncomfortable for some conservative sensibilities, but it is necessary. When you are the target of a moral indictment based on a tissue of lies, there is no way to defend yourself without calling into question the moral credentials of your attackers.

The war that Democrats have declared on America's social contract is a war on individual rights and individual accountability, which are the bedrock of America's constitutional system. The stakes in this war are enormous. Democrats' emphasis on group identities and group rights and progressives' clamoring for "social justice" will lead inexorably to a collectivist tyranny. This is a fight for American freedom–the soul of what this country stands for and the foundation of all its success.

4

The Democrats' Wars on Men and Women

WHATEVER PAGE ONE TURNS to in the Democratic playbook, one is reminded that Democrats regard politics as war by other means. In war, there are no rules, and Democrats have shown over and over that they are prepared to conduct that war with all the ruthlessness they can muster. In the 2016 election, their candidate was the first woman to be nominated for president by a national party—a fact they made one of the two pillars of their campaign. The other pillar was a campaign to demonize her Republican opponent as an insulter and abuser of women. They framed it as another sordid chapter in Republicans' perennial "war on women." Democrats were not fazed by the fact that their candidate's husband was an actual woman-abuser, not a rhetorical one like Trump, and that he had been accused of rape and was impeached and stripped of his law license for lying to a grand jury about a sexual act he had demanded a state employee perform when he was Arkansas's governor. At the time, because he was a Democrat, feminists like Gloria Steinem gave him a pass, claiming, "It's only sex." When the Republican House impeached Clinton for his abuses, Democrats—to a man and woman—rallied to support him.

The Democrats' indictment of Republicans for conducting a war on women is quite familiar. At the Democratic convention in 2012, Reuters reported that "two dozen Democratic women from the U.S. House of Representatives brought the charge that Republicans are waging a 'war on women,' to the Party's convention stage on Tuesday with sharp denunciations of Republicans on healthcare, equal pay and domestic violence." The congresswomen were led by then House Speaker Nancy Pelosi.[1] Sixteen years earlier, New York governor Mario Cuomo warned delegates to the 1996 Democratic convention that "the Republicans are the real threat. They are the real threat to our women."[2] The same ludicrous charge has resurfaced every presidential election year since.

In 2016, the political issue around which Democrats organized their assault on Republicans' character and moral decency was the alleged gender-wage gap (also a familiar charge). Under this alleged gap, Democrats claim that women are paid 24 cents less on the dollar than men for the same work and the same skills, merely because they are women. Democrats have even created an "Equal Pay Day" to dramatize the gap. In a speech on "Equal Pay Day" during her primary campaign, Clinton called for more transparency laws to ensure that women get equal pay and linked the issue to Democrats' push for a hike in the minimum wage because women are disproportionately represented in minimum-wage jobs. "We need to elevate this issue," she said as she pointed to the fact that multimillionaire male athletes make more than their female counterparts.[3] What she failed to mention is that because of their performances, male athletes generally draw far larger paying audiences to their events. In other words, they *earned* their bonus thanks to their individual talents rather than their group identity as males. Demanding equality of results for belonging to a politically favored gender is the antithesis of what America has hitherto been about. But this is what the Democrats' agenda calls for.

According to Clinton and the Democrats, women across America are being paid only 76 cents on the dollar compared to men.[4] This is demonstrably false, and Democrats know it, but they persist in citing it anyway. In fact, the government already *requires* employers to provide equal pay for equal work and has done so for the last 60 years—since the passage of the Equal Pay Act in 1963.[5] If it were true that women are paid 24 cents less on the dollar than men merely because they are women, employers would fire their male employees, hire women, and increase their profits 24 percent—an astronomical gain by normal business standards. It doesn't happen because it isn't true. It's just another case of Democrats being practiced liars with statistics and not being willing to correct their falsehoods when confronted with the truth. And they are not fearful of being exposed because of their lock on a supine media network. So their gullible supporters remain wedded to the falsehood that the clamor for "equal pay for equal work" advances their agenda and hastens the progressive future. Meanwhile, Republicans are generally too tongue-tied to call them out on it—to confront them as the liars they are.

Why aren't Republicans angry enough to shout this from the rooftops? Why don't they complain about the Democrats' *war on men*? Accusing men of stealing wages from women is an indictment of an entire gender. It's sexist. Why don't Republicans say so? Why don't they attack the hypocrisy of Democrats like Clinton for running their own gender-wage gap against women? After all, if you are willing to break the law, as the Clintons so clearly are, why should the Equal Pay Act stop you? Among the documents released with the WikiLeaks hacks was a 2015 e-mail by Clinton Foundation staffer Karuna Seshasai, who subsequently went to work for the Clinton presidential campaign. Seshasai's e-mail revealed the existence of a huge wage gap between men and women working for the Clinton Foundation—far more than 24 cents on the dollar: "Avg salary of the highest paid men is $294,157.50, while the avg salary of the highest paid women is $181,576.66 ($112K difference)," she wrote. "Median salary of the highest paid men is $346,106, while the median salary of the highest paid women is $185,386 ($190K difference)."[6] Why haven't Republicans called for an investigation of the Clinton Foundation for violating the provisions of the 1963 Equal Pay Act?

Republicans should be excoriating the Democrats for the number of women their policies have forced out of the labor force during the last eight years, or the number of women their policies have thrown into poverty, or the increased number of women on food stamps and on welfare, or the thousands of women who have been raped by illegal aliens because of the Democrats' failure to secure America's borders. Talk about the abuse of women!

The strategy is to put Democrats on the defensive by taking away their moral high ground. The strategy is to focus on the groups—races, genders, ethnicities, and classes—that suffer under their policies and rule. The goal is to expose their hypocrisy in posing as champions of the voiceless, the powerless, and oppressed.

5

Obstructionism Is a Good Thing If the Policies Are Bad

IN BUDGET FIGHTS AND in votes over Obamacare and other legislative programs, Democrats accuse Republicans of being obstructionists. The tactic works, intimidating them sufficiently to make them relent and allow the Democrats to prevail. Republicans back off because they fear the negative reviews in the Democrat-dominated press and a loss of support from the voting public when the Democrats begin accusing them of taking away programs that benefit women, minorities, and the poor. In the short run—and in the absence of a counterattack—Republicans may suffer from saying no, but in surrendering these battles over and over, they lose the war.

Andrew McCarthy has provided a sobering thought exercise for Republicans who think a submarine mentality is the way to win the political war:

> To illustrate the emptiness of arguments by apologists for the Republican Congress, one need only ask what would happen if the roles were reversed. What if a Republican president tried to rein in entitlement spending? What if he unilaterally announced that, in an exercise of "prosecutorial discretion," tax evasion laws would not be enforced to collect corporate taxes above ten percent of income? What if his IRS targeted progressive activists and his Justice Department stonewalled congressional investigations—including one involving a case in which an inane law-enforcement tactic (e.g., gun-walking) got a federal agent killed? We needn't tarry long on this. A Democratic Congress would throw down the gauntlet and risk a government shutdown in order to force the president to back down. A Democratic Congress would not hesitate to impeach the IRS commissioner and the attorney general; and it would relish impeaching the president himself—calculating that even if Democrats lost, they would leave the president battered and impotent.[1]

Republican voters elected a Republican Congress with record majorities in the House to say *no* to the Obama agenda. When Republicans caved to the Democratic juggernaut, they lost their most important asset—their base—and they left Obama unscathed. McCarthy continues: "Democrats do not tell their supporters, 'The president has veto power and Republicans have the numbers to block us, so don't expect us to accomplish anything.' Democrats know you move public opinion by fighting, even if you lose battles along the way. A movement has to *move*. And since they and the mainstream media are part of the same movement, they do not doubt their ability ultimately to turn public opinion in their favor."[2]

It's not capitulation in a particular battle that costs Republicans support from their own ranks; it's the capitulations over time that encourage their opponents and weaken their support. It's the message that the failure to say *no*—and to say it over and over—communicates.

> Democrats and the media care more about the advancement of their cause than Republicans care about preserving the Constitution. Democrats used every trick in the book to enact Obamacare, knowing it was immensely unpopular and would become even more unpopular as it gradually failed. They were willing to sacrifice themselves to short-term political damage in order to secure the long-term achievement of government-controlled healthcare. They understood that once Obamacare was on the books, the trajectory toward a single-payer system would be in place, and Republicans—for all their saber-rattling—would not defund it. Any future "fixes" would occur under Obamacare's assumptions about the government's preeminent regulatory role. The left is willing to take its hits on something so crucial to its cause.[3]

Because of their conviction that these battles are crucial to their "societal transformation," Democrats have made themselves masters of obstruction. For a hundred and more years, the Senate used its "advise and consent" role in ratifying Supreme Court nominations to pass only on a nominee's judicial qualifications, expertise in the law, and judicial character and temperament. But once the Democrats became a sufficiently left-wing party in the 1980s, Democrats on the Senate Judiciary Committee came prepared to blow up the proceedings to prevent the appointment of a justice who did not share their ideological views. A landmark case in this development was the aborted nomination of Judge Robert Bork to the court, who became a target of vilification and character assassination unprecedented in the annals of these nominations. The attack on Bork became a precedent for Democrats opposed to Republican nominees. The high-tech lynching of Clarence Thomas on the basis of an unproven private conversation he was alleged to have had with a Yale-educated civil rights lawyer 10 years in the past was so vicious and damaging that he was almost rejected, eventually gaining the nomination by a mere four votes. By contrast, when a rank ideologue of the left, Ruth Bader Ginsburg, was nominated by President Clinton, she was walked through the Senate by Republican Orrin Hatch and was approved by 94 out of 100 Senate votes.

When only one side is obstructing, the scales inevitably tip in its favor. If Republicans care about the Constitution, they have to find the courage to say *no* or lose their constituencies and ultimately their cause. They have to say *no* to the anticonstitutional views of Supreme Court nominees such as Ruth Bader Ginsburg and Sonia Sotomayor and to un-Constitutional executive orders by presidents like Barack

Obama, and that means they have to be prepared to obstruct them by any constitutional means necessary. Nor should they be cowed by a corrupt anti-Republican press. No candidate was ever vilified more by the media than Donald Trump, and he won.

6

Ending Leftist Indoctrination in Our Schools

THE SOCIETAL TRANSFORMATION THAT progressives hope to engineer begins in our universities and schools. No institution has been more instrumental in laying the groundwork for this transformation, and training its agents, than the American university. For nearly half a century, leftists have been working to turn liberal arts colleges into indoctrination and recruitment centers for left-wing causes. And they have succeeded. A 2016 article in the *Washington Post* reports,

> Millennials are the only age group in America in which a majority views socialism favorably. A national Reason-Rupe survey found that 53 percent of Americans under 30 have a favorable view of socialism compared with less than a third of those over 30.

> Moreover, Gallup has found that an astounding 69 percent of millennials say they'd be willing to vote for a "socialist" candidate for president—among their parents' generation, only a third would do so. Indeed, national polls and exit polls reveal about 70 to 80 percent of young Democrats are casting their ballots for presidential candidate Bernie Sanders, who calls himself a "democratic socialist."[1]

The change in the academic curriculum began in 1969 with the introduction of new fields that were the direct result of political pressures and lacked any tradition of scholarly standards. For example, the first Black Studies departments—later renamed African American Studies—were created as the result of a strike that shut down San Francisco State University and the occupation of the Cornell administration building by black militants carrying loaded shotguns. The Cornell militants demanded the creation of a Black Studies field and department, along with the right to appoint its professors and determine its curriculum. These demands were granted by a cowardly liberal administration, setting a trend throughout the university system and shaping the orientation of the field ever since.

"Ethnic" studies departments for Chicanos, Asians, gays, and lesbians quickly followed and became integral to the curriculum. The new fields celebrated their subjects and decried their allegedly systemic oppression by America and its white majority. Indeed, so rigidly did they follow the left-wing script that students refer to them generally as "Oppression Studies." Some schools, like Brandeis, have even created departments of "Social Justice," where left-wing professors instruct students in the evils of the American system and the virtues of the progressive worldview. The exception to the basic pattern (though not its oppression model) is the field of "Whiteness Studies," whose "scholarship" is dedicated to the examination of "white skin privilege" and "white supremacy" and the injustices committed by whites against "people of color."[2]

Because women are a majority in the academy and virtually every academic faculty in the liberal arts has one or several feminist professors, Women's Studies has had the greatest influence on the curriculum. In keeping with the principles of the new academic world, the Women's Studies curriculum is not governed by the principles of disinterested scholarly inquiry but rather by a political mission: to teach students to be radical feminists—to teach them that a patriarchy oppresses them. The preamble to the constitution adopted by the Women's Studies Association makes this agenda clear: "Women's Studies owes its existence to the movement for the liberation of women; the feminist movement exists because women are oppressed. Women's studies, diverse as its components are, has at its best shared a vision of a world free not only from sexism but also from racism, class-bias, ageism, heterosexual bias—from all the ideologies and institutions that have consciously or unconsciously oppressed and exploited some for the advantage of others."[3] This is a political program, not the description of a scholarly inquiry.

The linking of alleged oppressions—racism, sexism, ageism—now has an academic name, *intersectionality*, which sums up the ideological agenda of these academic activists. It was coined in 1989 by racial extremist Kimberle Williams

Crenshaw. According to Wikipedia, "It is the study of overlapping or *intersecting* social identities and related systems of oppression, domination, or discrimination. The theory suggests that—and seeks to examine how—various biological, social and cultural categories such as gender, race, class, ability, sexual orientation, religion, caste, age, nationality and other sectarian axes of identity interact on multiple and often simultaneous levels. . . . This framework can be used to understand how systemic injustice and social inequality occur on a multidimensional basis."[4]

Obviously, an approach that assumes at the outset not only that there is the oppression of these groups individually but that all these oppressions are interrelated is not a scholarly or even academic approach to the subject but an ideological script with political consequences. Because of the all-encompassing mandate of fields like Black Studies and Women's Studies, the courses they offer have expansive subjects that take in large swathes of a student's education and are taught by ideologues rather than scholars. For example, courses on "global feminism" focus on the evils of the international capitalist economic system but are taught by professors whose academic credentials are not in economics or even sociology or political science but in comparative literature, education, and Women's Studies.[5] To say that our universities now engage in systematic miseducation and indoctrination would be an understatement. All that matters from an academic point of view, as currently practiced, is that the analysis conforms to the progressive orthodoxy. The University of California, Santa Cruz, for example, features a seminar on "how to make a revolution"—hardly a scholarly inquiry—and then explains that the revolution is to be “antiracist” and “anticapitalist.”[6] And this is a public university supported by taxpayers.

These ideological programs have spread their tentacles throughout the contemporary university, so they encompass not only academic courses but “centers” and “institutes” to carry on the work and propaganda of the left. The University of California, Berkeley, hosts a Center for Race and Gender, for example, which includes an “Islamophobia Studies” program, although Islam is neither a race nor a gender. Evidently the leftist administrators of the center felt that Islamophobia—a term invented by the Muslim Brotherhood—was a problem and decided to give it support. The Islamophobia Studies program publishes the *Islamophobia Studies Journal* and an annual Islamophobia “report,” which targets critics of Islamic terrorism as Islamophobes in an effort to discredit their work.[7] Like everything else at the University of California, these “studies” are funded by California taxpayers, who imagine they are supporting scholarly inquiries and research.

The transformation of the academic curriculum into an indoctrination program for the political left has been made possible by the steady purge of Republicans from academic faculties over the last 50 years. The Klein study of 7,243 professors in economics, law, psychology, history, and journalism/communication at the 40 top-rated universities found that 66 of 170 departments surveyed had no Republican faculty members at all. Zero.[8] This development violates the fundamental precepts of academic scholarship and academic freedom, which were designed to maintain a skeptical attitude toward ideological certainties and look askance at attempts to indoctrinate students. The classic statement on the subject is the "Declaration of the Principles on Academic Freedom and Academic Tenure," published in 1915 by the American Association of University Professors, which clearly states: "It is not the function of a faculty member in a democracy to indoctrinate his/her students with ready-made conclusions on controversial subjects. The faculty member is expected to train students to think for themselves, and to provide them access to those materials, which they need if they are to think intelligently. Hence, in giving instruction upon controversial matters the faculty member is expected to be of a fair and judicial mind, and to set forth justly, without supercession or innuendo, the divergent opinions of other investigators."[9]

In other words, the function of an education in a democratic society is to teach students how to think, not to tell them what to think, as authoritarian systems do. If one wants to understand the leftward shift of the Democratic Party and the leftward drift in the culture at large, one need look no further than the political subversion of our universities.

It is what Republicans and conservatives have *allowed* to happen by ceding America's schools to the left. How many battles have Republicans lost because of this miseducation of America's youth at the hands of ideologues posing as professors? Any effort to stop the left's plan for a societal transformation must begin with measures to restore universities to the institutions they once were—to see to it that liberal arts faculties adhere to the same nonideological standards as the sciences and that faculties once again feature diverse political perspectives that reflect the diversity of society at large. Unless Republicans are prepared to do this, the hill they must climb to reach future electorates will grow steeper and steeper, and the progressives' plan to "fundamentally transform the United States of America" will proceed apace.[10]

In fact, the means to accomplish a reform of the universities is ready to hand. The left has already created a vast diversity apparatus at virtually all accredited institutions of higher education. The diversity offices at these universities have budgets running into the millions and operate in accord with a mission statement similar to this one at Yale:

> This office was established with the premise that expanding diversity within the university enhances the educational experience and furthers the understanding of the entire scholarly community. An atmosphere of civility and mutual respect towards difference is indispensable to the educational process and enables the free interchange of ideas that is the basis of scholarship. These differences may be immutable or changeable, cultural, ethnic, religious, *intellectual, ideological, or political.* Each of these qualities is integral to the identity we form as individuals, and all are essential to creating a vibrant university community composed of individuals with unique perspectives and backgrounds. The university must commit itself to a policy of inclusion, respect for difference, and fairness, and guarantee the same rights and freedoms to all its members to ensure the fullest degree of intellectual freedom.[11]

The italicized words affirming the value of intellectual, ideological, and political diversity do not appear in the Yale diversity statement or in the diversity statement of any other school. If they did, and if universities were prepared to pursue this kind of diversity—essential to an institution of higher learning and crucial to the health of a democracy—if they were prepared to recruit the underrepresented political, ideological, and intellectual elements of the community that supports them, the current problem would begin to correct itself. But there is no will to do this, obviously, or the problem would not have reached its present appalling state.

Therefore, Republicans should make it their business to persuade university administrators to see the wisdom of having the institutions that shape America's future generations be less adversarial toward the community that supports them and more reflective of the diversity that characterizes them. Eighty-five percent of American college students attend public universities that are supported by taxpayers and funded by state governments. As of 2014, Republicans controlled 68 out of 98 partisan state legislative chambers—the highest number in the history of the party. In other words, Republicans control the purse strings that can be used to restrain the progressive juggernaut. Why should half the country fund institutions that regard them as racists, sexists, homophobes, Islamophobes, and xenophobes—in a word, "deplorables"? Republicans should use their leverage to represent the half of the population that academic ideologues have put into the basket of deplorables and restore intellectual diversity to institutions that have become one-party states. Republicans should use their leverage to restore academic standards and democratic values to the most important institutions shaping America's future.

A call from the chair of an appropriations or education committee asking university presidents in his or her state to put the italicized words *intellectual, ideological, or political* into their diversity missions is the way to begin the process. Republicans should ask for the university presidents' commitments to correct the gross underrepresentation of their party on his faculties. Professors should not be hired *because* they are Republicans, but they should not be excluded—as they are now—*because* they are Republicans. Universities should find a way to recruit scholars who happen to be Republicans until there is a reasonable balance, one that would reassure the public that the current discrimination against Republicans is ended. Universities should conduct inquiries as to how this state of affairs has come to pass and introduce procedural changes to make sure that there is no such political bias against Republicans and conservatives in the future.

The appropriations or education chairs of state legislatures should ask university presidents to set goals for hiring underrepresented faculty and to conduct an annual review on their progress. They should ask university presidents to task their offices of diversity with seeing that underrepresented textbooks by conservative authors are no longer excluded from required reading lists, from which they are now almost entirely absent. Offices of diversity should also be tasked with seeing that there is appropriate balance in the speakers who are invited to campus, in the often substantial fees they are offered, and in the university resources that are generally provided to faculty and students to put on public affairs events.

There will be no progress on this front unless Republican legislatures are prepared to go to the wall to see that these recommendations are acted upon and to do so with the same vigor and commitment that Democrats would if the roles were reversed. Democrats will attack these proposals with the same vicious slanders they use to attack all Republican proposals that threaten their progressive agendas. They will say these Republican proposals are an attack on academic freedom, for example. In fact, it is the progressive left that has destroyed the academic freedom and intellectual diversity that once reigned on college campuses. Republicans cannot afford to cave in to these attacks and continue to allow the left to use the trillion-dollar structures of the university system as a political base to destroy the society that created them.

The problem of America's schools is at the heart of the destructive changes to American society and culture over the last few decades, and it does not stop with higher education. The problem in our K–12 schools is not much better, and since its students are younger, it is in many cases worse. Here is a typical testimony from a student, now in college:

> At my high school, I cannot recall hearing a conservative opinion expressed by a teacher, despite the fact that I lived in a conservative swath of north San Diego county. My teachers were almost entirely Democrats, and were vocal about their beliefs. I was told by my Chemistry teacher that a single-payer healthcare was the only "fair" system. I had a World History teacher tell us that the natural and best way for society to progress was to turn to communism. Not Cuban Communism, or Soviet Communism, but "true Communism," because the Soviets just didn't implement it correctly,

> we were taught. I even had an English teacher who forced us to spend three months analyzing writing through a Marxist lens, because apparently we "have spent our whole lives hearing about capitalism."[12]

Behind this deplorable state of affairs lie the education schools at our universities, which have redefined their mission, and hence the mission of the teachers they train, as pursuing "social justice." An entire series of texts designed for teacher instruction and published by the Columbia Teachers College is devoted to "teaching social justice" in mathematics and other unlikely subjects.[13] Its editor is Obama collaborator and unrepentant terrorist William Ayers.

In this area too, Republicans have abdicated their responsibility to protect the integrity of our democratic institutions and have provided the left with another taxpayer-supported avenue to shape the minds of American youth. This can be more easily remedied than the situation in higher education, provided Republicans have the will to do so. Superintendents of school districts should draw up a Hatch Act for teachers to prevent them from insinuating political agendas into the classroom. Teachers can teach controversial issues but should be barred from taking sides on such matters or extruding partisan politics into the classroom. Teachers who do so should risk suspension and the possible loss of their teaching licenses.

But it is all in the will. Do Republicans have the will to fight these battles and win them?

7

Fixing the Political Universe That Doesn't Exist

THE IRS CODE 501c3 designates qualifying institutions as "charitable foundations," exempting them from paying taxes so long as they are "nonpolitical." But are they? Recently, it was announced that a group of "liberal" tax-exempt foundations, including George Soros's Open Society Foundations and the Ford Foundation, pledged more than $100 million to the racist, antipolice, riot-fomenting organization Black Lives Matter, also a 501c3.[1]

The Ford Foundation is a $12-billion organization whose official mission is to "advance human welfare." This is virtually identical to the government's own constitutionally defined mission. But because the government's budget is encumbered by obligations like the national debt and entitlements, it has been estimated that the Ford Foundation actually has more discretionary income than the federal government. Its broad mission, like the government's, provides Ford with a mandate to influence, shape, and underwrite policies and programs that affect every aspect of American society. Under IRS rules, Ford funds tax-exempt "think tanks" that hire experts to develop policies and then lobby legislatures to get taxpayers to fund them. Ford and scores of other tax-exempt foundations, think tanks, and health advocacy groups were involved in architecting the Affordable Care Act, otherwise known as "Obamacare," and then in lobbying the public and the Congress to pass it.[2] The range of the influence—the *political* influence—of these tax-exempt entities extends from health, to immigration, to environmental and national security policies, and in fact through the entire range of issues with which government is concerned. In other words, every aspect of the progressive agenda is advanced through organizations and institutions that the IRS designates as charitable and tax-exempt.

These tax-exempt entities are divided into funding institutions like Ford and policy/advocacy groups like Black Lives Matter and the American Civil Liberties Union, which used its tax-exempt funds to draw up the Sanctuary Cities pledge of noncooperation with the Department of Homeland Security's mission to keep illegal aliens and terrorists out of the country. The entire so-called rights coalition, which includes the ACLU, NARAL, the NAACP, MALDEF, Planned Parenthood, and a hundred similar left-wing groups that lobby and campaign to push the Democratic Party farther to the left on their issues, is composed of organizations that fall under the

501c3 IRS code. Many of these organizations, like the ACLU, Planned Parenthood, and the NAACP, have non-tax-exempt arms too, so they can openly conduct partisan political campaigns, even with the same personnel.

The left-wing funding organizations, of which Ford is the largest, have assets in excess of $100 billion, or more than 10 *times* greater than the assets of conservative foundations.[3] On the other hand, the gap really gets huge when one looks at the policy think tanks and advocacy groups for which Ford and the others provide the funding.

As of 2012, there were 117 progressive 501c3s that devoted more than 50 percent of their program activities to supporting open borders or citizen rights for illegal aliens. There were only 9 conservative 501c3s to oppose these same agendas. The total annual revenues of the progressive immigration groups—the funds they received annually from progressive foundations and individual donors to spend on advocacy—amounted to $306.1 million, while the revenues available to conservative groups was only $13.8 million. In other words, the total funds annually available to the left for advocacy to promote open-borders agendas were more than 22 *times* greater than the total funds available to conservatives to oppose them.[4]

The imbalance is even worse in regard to other issues central to the progressive agenda. As of 2012, there were 553 environmental 501c3s dedicated to promoting the left's environmental causes like global warming and its solutions—more government controls. There were only 32 conservative groups to oppose them and promote market-friendly approaches to environmental problems. The net assets of the progressive environmental groups totaled $9.53 *billion* compared to $38.2 million in net assets of the conservative groups. This amounted to a progressive advantage in environmental lobbying of 249 to 1. The annual grants awarded by the 32 conservative groups to environment-related issues totaled $1.2 million. The annual grants awarded by the 553 progressive environmental groups totaled $555.4 million. In other words, progressive grants to promote their environmental agenda were almost 462 times greater than their political opponents.[5]

Why haven't Republicans done something about this monstrous advantage provided to the left by the current tax code to shape what government does and does not do? To rectify this situation does not require rocket science. The loophole that allows this inequitable and destructive situation to exist is obvious. The IRS defines "political" as activities on behalf of electoral candidates and political parties. By regarding everything else (so long as it is not profitable or to someone's personal benefit) as "charitable," the IRS provides a cover and funding base to enterprises that are evidently not charitable. Hospitals available to help all people in need are charitable. Organizations devoted to encouraging illegal aliens to break American laws are not.

The existence of these tax-exempt organizations with massive amounts of money behind them disenfranchises American voters. If the Ford Foundation has billions available to devise public policies and then persuade legislators that they are sound, what does that do to the interests and preferences of individual voters whom these legislators are supposed to represent?

Instead of planting their heads in the sand, as they have for decades, Republicans should be demanding revisions to the tax code and redefining charities to be institutions like hospitals and adoption services that exist for the benefit of everyone and not just political factions. Nonprofits concerned with policy and political issues should not be getting subsidies from the taxpayers; truly charitable institutions should. Congress should also pass legislation sunsetting tax-exempt funding foundations—whatever their purposes—within 5 to 10 years of their creation. The Ford Foundation has been criticized by the Ford family for departing from the intentions of its founder and for attacking the capitalist system that created its wealth. Many similar foundations pursue policies that bear no relation to the intentions of their founders. Yet they exist in perpetuity, receiving annual subsidies from a public that has no say in their directions.

The remedy is to terminate them after the founding generation dies out. Older foundations like Ford should be sunset immediately and its funds distributed to hospitals and other institutions that serve the needy and the poor, recipients for whom the word "charity" was invented. As the tax law is presently designed, the Ford Foundation will exist forever and will be accountable to no one except a self-perpetuating board, which is accountable to no one. This is undemocratic and unacceptable. Republicans have ignored the problems created by this system for far too long. Unless they are prepared to get serious about fighting the war the left has declared, unless the powers of this shadow political universe are checked, the progressives' march toward a societal transformation cannot be arrested, let alone stopped.

8

Government Unions

A Conflict of Interest That Needs to Be Ended

Among the forces of the left pushing the progressive agenda, few are more politically powerful than government unions like SEIU, AFSCME, and the National Education Association, which is the largest labor union in the United States. These government unions are the most important funding base of the Democratic Party and provide the lion's share of its troops. Government unions spend hundreds of millions of dollars every year supporting the Democratic Party and its electoral campaigns and agitating for their cause: for bigger government and higher taxes to expand their labor pool and increase its benefits. Their radical leadership was on full display in 2011 when Wisconsin governor Scott Walker, who was facing a state budget crisis, attempted to rein in their excesses. Walker proposed a "budget repair bill" that would limit their collective bargaining rights to wages, ask government workers to pay slightly more for their existing health care and pension benefits, and give union members the right to decide every year whether they wanted to belong to a union or not. The bill was also designed to end the process by which union dues were automatically deducted from state employees' paychecks, depriving them of the freedom to say no.

The unions responded by dispatching 5,000 of their members—teachers, prison guards, and other public-sector employees—to descend on the Wisconsin capitol, barricade themselves inside, and foment a riot. Union goons broke windows and shouted threats of physical violence at legislators who had to pass through their gauntlet to do the work that Wisconsin voters had elected them to do. Walker was called a "fascist," as were other Republican lawmakers. The unions also mounted a campaign of harassment and intimidation throughout the state. Businesses that failed to back their opposition to Walker's bill were threatened with public boycotts.[1] One disgruntled teachers' union member sent death threats to 15 Republican legislators, in which she chillingly warned, "Please put your things in order because you will be killed and your families will also be killed due to your actions in the last 8 weeks."[2] Republican state senator Glenn Grothman received a note under his office door that read, "THE ONLY GOOD Republican is a DEAD Republican."[3] To block a vote on the bill by preventing a quorum, Democratic legislators fled the state and went into hiding. The disruptions in the capitol lasted three weeks. Damage resulting from the union-led riots came to nearly $8 million.[4] As a result of his battles with the government unions, Governor Walker had to withstand two recall votes. Only his fortitude made it possible to thwart the unions' attempt to nullify the wishes of the Wisconsin voters who had elected him.

While government unions are the fastest-growing sector of a labor movement otherwise in decline, they are a fairly recent phenomenon. As late as 1960, there was not a single recognized union in the federal government. This absence was due to the fact that most politicians, and indeed most labor leaders, originally opposed collective bargaining in the public sector as an impossible conflict of interest and a threat to public safety. Although a supporter of private-sector unions, President Franklin Roosevelt opposed unions for government workers. In 1937, Roosevelt insisted that "meticulous attention should be paid to the special relations and obligations of public servants to the public itself and to the Government. . . . The process of collective bargaining, as usually understood, cannot be transplanted into the public service."[5]

The ability of government unions to act politically represents an unacceptable conflict of interest. Government unions can raise slush funds for candidates and elect those who promise to raise their member's wages and provide them with lucrative benefit packages paid for by taxpayers. Pensions for government workers wrung as concessions from politicians afraid to resist their demands, however unreasonable, are today one of the most crushing burdens on local and state governments. At the same time, the justification for government unions is not at all obvious, since government workers, unlike workers in the private sector, can vote to retire officials who treat them unfairly.

Not surprisingly, since the leaders of government unions are far to the political left, labor expert Matthew Vadum has observed,

> The labor movement's reigning ideology has changed dramatically over the decades. Seventy-five years ago, organized labor was a strongly patriotic force, and so allergic to radicalism that it purged its ranks of the communists who had secretly been trying to seize control of its movement. Today's unions are run almost exclusively by left-wing radicals, socialists, and communists. Lane Kirkland, the AFL-CIO leader who collaborated with President Ronald Reagan in providing assistance to Poland's Solidarity movement and in other anticommunist causes, would likely turn over in his grave at the behavior of his successors, John Sweeney and Richard Trumka. Embracing the use of anti-American rhetoric in setting out their foreign and domestic policy positions, Sweeney and Trumka helped government unions transform the labor movement into a stalking horse for leftism.[6]

That there has been no Republican legislation to outlaw government unions and restore the democratic system to health is another result of Republican Party fecklessness and its failure to take seriously the stakes should the left's agenda prevail. Yet there are courageous Republicans like Scott Walker who have demonstrated the will to stand up to them. Perhaps his example will inspire other Republicans to do likewise.

9

Corruption and Cowardice

BILL AND HILLARY CLINTON left the White House in 2000, "broke" by their own account. By the time Hillary launched her campaign for the presidency in 2016, they were together worth $100 million, though neither had a real job other than her government position as secretary of state or his as an official of the Clinton Foundation, which they created in 1997 and which became the ex-president's chief vehicle when he left the White House. The Clinton Foundation is a $2-billion tax-exempt 501c3 that has thrived on donations from individuals, corporate enterprises, and foreign governments, many seeking favors from Hillary Clinton when she was secretary of state. Such paid favors to foreigners is forbidden by law, which the foundation helped the Clintons to circumvent. In fact, the majority of the private individuals and companies who were granted access to Secretary of State Clinton were donors to the Clinton Foundation or lined the Clintons' pockets by giving them astronomical fees—hundreds of thousands of dollars—for a single speech or meeting. This added up to millions in income annually and explains how they were able to enter the ranks of the nation's richest Americans in such a short time. The vast majority of the Clinton Foundation's expenditures are not in the form of charitable grants. The standard for 501c3 fund-granting institutions is about 75 percent of overall expenditures for charitable donations; the figure for the Clinton Foundation is 10–15 percent. The rest is allocated to salaries, travel, administrative costs, and activities that could be political or not.

Hillary Clinton was quite aware of the impropriety of the operations of the Clinton Foundation. She was so determined to prevent others from looking at its relationships and internal functions that she took the momentous step of hiding her official correspondence from the public by putting them on a private nongovernment, nonsecure server. This enabled her to circumvent the stipulations of the Freedom of Information Act requiring transparency of government officials. In taking this step, she knowingly violated multiple provisions of the Espionage Act and exposed hundreds of thousands of e-mails, including many that contained classified and top-secret information about the government she swore to serve and protect, to America's enemies around the world.

This risk seemed necessary to her because she was also aware that the lines that she, her husband, and the Clinton staff regularly crossed to serve their political and personal aggrandizement agendas exposed them to prosecution under multiple laws other than the Espionage Act. These illegalities and problematic conflicts of interest were visible in the activities of Huma Abedin, Hillary's Deputy Chief of Staff at the State Department. Abedin was employed simultaneously by the foundation and the Teneo Group, a global business advisory firm and investment bank whose mission was to make the Clintons rich.

One of the hacked documents released by WikiLeaks was a memo from Teneo's CEO, Doug Band. The memo was written to John Podesta, head of the Center for American Progress, a 501c3 brain trust for the Democratic Party and subsequently chairman of Hillary Clinton's presidential campaign. In the memo, Band explains:

> We have in effect served as agents, lawyers, managers and implementers to secure speaking, business and advisory service deals [for Bill Clinton]. In support of the President's for-profit activity, we also have solicited and obtained, as appropriate, in-kind services for the President and his family—for personal travel, hospitality, vacation and the like. Neither Justin nor I are separately compensated for these activities (e.g., we do not receive a fee for, or percentage of, the more than $50 million in for-profit activity we have personally helped to secure for President Clinton to date or the $66 million in future contracts, should he choose to continue with those engagements).[1]

Band's concern about the selling of influence by the Clintons and himself—in other words, the graft involved in the complex relationship between Secretary of State Clinton, her husband, the Clinton Foundation, and Teneo—was voiced in a second e-mail, dated November 12, 2011, and addressed to Clinton and her attorney, Cheryl Mills, along with Huma Abedin: "I'm starting to worry that if this story gets out we're screwed."[2]

The question is, why didn't it get out, and why weren't they screwed? Why did it take a WikiLeaks hack of internal e-mails and memos to uncover this corruption at the highest levels of government and involving a secretary of state who shaped America's foreign policy? It's not as though Bill Clinton was a secret agent or the Clinton Foundation and its enabler, Teneo, institutions that were cloaked in secrecy. Why did Republicans conduct no investigations into the operations of the Clinton Foundation in the six years they controlled both houses of Congress, when such an investigation would have changed the whole tenor of the 2016 presidential election, affecting the shape of things for years to come?

One answer is that influence peddling, as Donald Trump complained throughout the election, is a way of life in Washington, and the fallout from such an inquiry could spread far beyond the Clintons. But a far more important reason is the familiar Republican failure of nerve, an unwillingness if the stakes seem high enough—if national security is involved, for example—to poke the hornets' nest.

Consider the case of Hillary Clinton's right-hand aide, Huma Abedin. Abedin was hired by Hillary from a previous job working for an organization run by the Muslim World League, the creator of al-Qaeda. Her boss, Abdullah Omar Nasseef, was Secretary General of the league, and is wanted by authorities in connection with the 9/11 attacks. Abedin's mother and brother are leaders of the Muslim Brotherhood, as was her late father.[3] She herself was a board member of the Muslim Students Association, a Muslim Brotherhood front group. During Hillary Clinton's tenure as secretary of state, the Obama administration threw its support to the Brotherhood, helping them come to power in Egypt and opposing the al-Sisi regime that subsequently overthrew them. A reasonable question would be, did Huma Abedin, Hillary's Deputy Chief of Staff at the State Department, influence America's tilt toward the Brotherhood during these turbulent events that affected America's policy and eroded America's power in the Middle East? Congresswoman Michelle Bachmann and four other House Republicans actually signed a letter to the Inspector General asking a series of questions to that effect, suggesting an inquiry was in order.

Note that only 5 Republicans out of more than 200 Republican House members were even willing to ask such questions. The reason became quickly obvious, as the letter was denounced by liberal media as a "witch-hunt," and the signers were attacked by fellow Republicans, including Speaker of the House John Boehner, who said: "I don't know Huma, but from everything that I do know of her she has a sterling character. And I think accusations like this being thrown around are pretty dangerous."[4] Abedin's collusion in the corruption of the Clinton Foundation and violations of the Espionage Act do not indicate a "sterling character" and seem potentially far more dangerous than asking questions. There were no accusations in the letter, only suggested inquiries, and reasonable ones at that. The five Republicans who thought these inquiries might be important for the nation's security and untold victims of future violence in the Middle East were sent to the congressional woodshed, where they were isolated by the Republican leadership.

Republicans need to ask themselves whether they are serious about the fate of their nation and whether they are willing to stand up and do something about it. Hundreds of thousands of people, including Americans, died in the Middle East because of the failure of the Obama-Clinton-Kerry policies supporting the Muslim Brotherhood and Iran, and millions became refugees. The stakes in these battles are high, and the casualties have already come home.

10

Party of the People

THE DEMOCRATIC PARTY IS powered by a view of itself that is immensely flattering and also false. Democrats see themselves as champions of the underdogs—of minorities, of the poor, of the middle class more recently, and of the oppressed in general. In their view, it is Republicans and the political right, with their corporate sponsors and big-money donors, who make up the party of the powerful and the rich, while Democrats and progressives defend the other "99 percent." Until the advent of Donald Trump, Republicans have helped this narrative by talking like accountants and focusing on tax relief, which Democrats—who seem to have no idea how jobs are actually created—can spin as defending the rich. At the Democrats' 2000 convention, while accepting his party's nomination, Al Gore summed up this outlook in a slogan: "They're for the powerful; we're for the people!"[1] In the 2016 presidential campaign, this same canard was ubiquitous as Hillary Clinton's mantra, which she repeated over and over, even in inappropriate places, as in her answer to a question about the Supreme Court during the third debate: "I feel strongly that the Supreme Court needs to stand on the side of the American people. Not on the side of the powerful corporations and the wealthy."[2]

This Democratic snake oil has a long and unpretty history. It was forged during the moderately populist and immoderately corrupt presidency of Andrew Jackson, spokesman for the "common man," who entered the White House as a self-proposed champion of the people battling the "moneyed elite." Both the image and the aura were transparent manipulations to seduce a willing public. Despite humble beginnings, Jackson was a man of means who, like the post–White House Clintons, basked in the privileges of an aristocratic life. The same comfortable circumstances did not discourage him from plundering the property of his political rivals, or justifying his avarice as a "sharing" of the wealth, or exploiting the morality play he had created to expand his personal power. Nor did Jackson's Everyman enthusiasms keep him from owning and selling slaves throughout his life or from presiding over the forced removal of American Indian tribes from their native lands on the "Trail of Tears."

Politics being a market in which fictions are currency, the Jacksonian myth established the enduring template of the two-party system. As a Republican newspaper in Tennessee complained at a time when the Democrats were the party of the segregated South, "The Democratic Party is [seen as] the poor man's party, and . . . the Republican Party is the party of boodle and corruption and they obtain and maintain their supremacy in all states by the undue use of money."[3]

The ability to see itself as a perennial underdog in a class war it regards as integral to capitalism is an abiding strength of the political left. But the image is unsupported by the facts. Far from being the party of the people, Democrats and their progressive core represent America's social and cultural elites and constitute the richest, most organized, and most economically powerful political force in American history. As Christopher Caldwell observed in a *New York Times* essay,

> The Democratic Party is the party to which elites *belong*. It is the party of Harvard (and most of the Ivy League), of Microsoft and Apple (and most of Silicon Valley), of Hollywood and Manhattan (and most of the media) and, although there is some evidence that numbers are evening out in this election cycle, of Goldman Sachs (and most of the investment banking profession). . . . The Democrats have the support of more, and more active, billionaires [than the Republicans]. Of the twenty richest ZIP codes in America, according to the Center for Responsive Politics, 19 gave the bulk of their money to the Democrats in the last election, in most cases the vast bulk—86% in 10024 on the Upper West Side.[4]

Wall Street—the very symbol of capitalist excess and wealth—was a key player in Barack Obama's successful presidential election run in 2008 and lined up again behind Hillary Clinton in 2016. Counterintuitive at first, this fact becomes immediately intelligible once one realizes that big government works for Wall Street bankers who float all the bonds that underwrite government spending programs and take their percentage on every dollar of big-government debt. Award-winning business reporter Charles Gasparino observes, "The assumption made by most Americans is that because investment bankers are rich they must favor Republicans because by definition Republicans favor lower taxes on the wealthy and on big business. And of course, while no one *likes* high taxes, what's more important than the tax rate is how much income you make in the first place: paying 30 percent of your money in taxes if you make a million dollars is better than paying a 20 percent tax rate on an income of only half a million."[5]

11

Go on the Attack and Stay on It

IRONICALLY, IT WAS A billionaire businessman who broke the mold in the 2016 presidential campaign and brought a new voice into Republican politics. Instead of focusing on taxes and regulations, Donald Trump took up the cause of the forgotten working class, promising to restore America's industrial prowess and bring back the jobs that a corrupt elite with a globalist outlook had negotiated away in reckless trade deals that sent Americans to the back of the bus and squandered the prosperity they had created over generations. The same globalism expressed in Hillary Clinton's "dream" of common markets and open borders had underwritten an invasion of illegal immigrants that was driving down American wages, destroying American sovereignty, and making

American citizens vulnerable to the violence of hundreds of thousands of criminals crossing into the country illegally.

Equally groundbreaking was Trump's bluntness in confronting the corruption of both parties for participating in a rigged system that left their constituencies out in the cold. The failure to secure the borders was a national disgrace in which both parties were complicit. In focusing on the hundreds of thousands of criminal aliens who had not been blocked at the borders and were not deported, he broke the silence imposed by the politically correct party line. In calling Clinton a "crook," a "liar," and the enabler of a sexual predator, he took her off the pedestal on which her gender and the Democrats' fantasy of a Republican "war on women" had placed her. The double standard that protected women while pretending to "empower" them was gone. She and her hypocrisies were no longer untouchable. By speaking out against the Democrats' rape of the inner cities and their treatment of their black constituents as second-class citizens, Trump burst a bubble that had protected Democrats from the consequences of their actions and opened the ranks of the Republican Party to "people of color."

Trump's readiness to go for the Democrats' jugular rallied Republican voters frustrated by their leaders' long-running deference to Democratic outrages and their willingness to keep their party on the defensive. It was this rallying of the Republican troops, who turned out in record crowds during the campaign, that led Trump to call what he had created a "movement." It is a movement, first of all, anchored in its opposition to the Democrats' collectivism and in defense of individual liberty. That is the meaning of Trump's early commitment to a list of Supreme Court nominees committed to a conservative view of the Constitution and his outspoken defense of the First and Second Amendments that guarantee America's freedoms.

Perhaps Trump's most significant innovation as a Republican candidate was the moral language he used to indict his Democratic opponent. Previously, Republicans would have been too polite to call their opponents liars and crooks—even when the evidence clearly showed that they were. If their opponent was a woman, they would never have dreamed of using such language, so deferential were they to the stringent rules of political correctness. Trump broke free of this constraint, and it is safe to say that political correctness will never have the stranglehold on public discourse that it once did. But Republicans need to take this a step further and create a unifying theme that has a moral resonance with which they can characterize their opponents and level the political playing field.

That theme is individual freedom. The economic redistribution that progressives demand is not "fairness," as they maintain. Socialism is theft and a war on individual freedom. Compulsory public schools are not a service to minorities and the poor but are infringements on their freedom to choose an education that will allow them to pursue the American dream. Obamacare is objectionable not only because its mandates drive up the costs and diminish the quality of health care, as Republicans have argued. Far more important is that government-controlled health care takes away the freedom of individuals to manage their own health and secure their life chances. Onerous taxes and massive government debt are not accounting problems; they are a war on the ability of individuals to work for themselves instead of the government and are therefore an attack on individual freedom. This is the moral language Republicans need to use if they are going to defeat the progressive agenda.

The movement galvanized by Trump can stop the progressive juggernaut and change the American future, but only if it emulates the strategy of his campaign: *Be on offense; take no prisoners; stay on the attack.* To stop the Democrats and their societal transformation, Republicans must adhere to a strategy that begins with a punch in the mouth. That punch must pack an emotional wallop large enough to throw them off balance and neutralize their assaults. It must be framed as a moral indictment that stigmatizes them in the way their attacks stigmatize Republicans. It must expose them for their hypocrisy. It must hold them accountable for the divisions they sow and the suffering they cause.

The first question to ask when thinking about how to frame such attacks is this: How is it possible that Democrats and progressives can pose as defenders of minorities, the middle class, and the poor? Democratic policies have devastated all three. "The data is going to indicate sadly," the left-winger Tavis Smiley admitted in a candid moment, "that when the Obama administration is over, black people will have lost ground in every single leading economic indicator category."[1] For generations, Democrats have controlled America's inner cities and virtually all the urban blight zones. Their policies have made it more difficult for law-abiding citizens to acquire guns to defend themselves and more difficult for police to apprehend predators and keep them off the streets. Their welfare policies have destroyed families and created lifelong dependencies on government handouts. The number of African American lives damaged or destroyed by Democratic policies alone would exceed the wildest dreams of any Klansman.

And it's not only African American lives. The progressive Obama administration has been directly responsible for creating more poverty than any administration since Jimmy Carter's. Forty-seven million Americans are on food stamps, and 100 million are receiving government handouts; 94 million Americans of working age have given up finding work and have left the labor force entirely. Yet Democrats are still able to persuade people that they are defenders of minorities, working Americans, and the poor.

How do they do it? Obviously not by helping minorities and the poor. They do it by *attacking* Republicans and the rich as uncaring and oppressive. They portray conservatives as the enemies of minorities and the poor and rich people as refusing to pay their "fair share." They portray their political opponents as racists. It is by demonizing conservatives and demonizing wealth that Democrats are able to pretend they are friends of minorities and the poor, even as they leave them mired in dependency and exploit them for political gain.

Conservatives habitually fail to appreciate the cynicism of these attacks. Democrats don't actually hate rich people or believe they are oppressors. Democratic Party socialists want to be rich and work overtime to achieve it, often—like the Clintons—exploiting a corrupt political system to do so. In fact, the really successful Democratic Party socialists *are* rich—filthy rich. Just ask George Soros, Jon Corzine, Nancy

Pelosi, Rahm Emanuel, Terry McAuliffe, and scores of other multimillionaire and billionaire progressives like them. As far as progressives are concerned, rich people are fine, provided they toe the party line and support its destructive agenda. This may be cynicism on steroids, but for them, it has been a winning strategy. By attacking Republicans as racists, Democrats show that they are friends of minorities; by attacking rich taxpayers as selfish, they show that they are friends of the poor. Never mind that minorities and the poor are worse off under their rule. Politically, the strategy works.

How can believers in individual rights and free markets expose this charade and repel the attacks? How can they neutralize the slanders and show that it is actually *conservatives* who defend opportunity and independence for minorities and the poor, for working Americans, and for the middle class? It's not rocket science: Republicans need to turn the Democrats' guns around and fight fire with fire.

12

A Postelection Agenda

THERE CAN BE NO "honeymoon" in the wake of this election—the most divisive since America's Civil War. Republicans must drop their attitude that these political conflicts are "business as usual" and must begin to confront the fact that the progressive agenda is a dagger aimed at the heart of America's social contract and the security of the American people. Two points in Trump's campaign speech at Gettysburg, which he called his "Contract with the American Voter," underscore this point. Trump pledged that on his first day in office, he would "begin removing the more than 2 million criminal illegal immigrants from the country and cancel visas to foreign countries that won't take them back," and he would "suspend immigration from terror-prone regions where vetting cannot safely occur. All vetting of people coming into our country will be considered extreme vetting."[1] The fact that Democrats had vigorously opposed both attempts to protect Americans, calling Trump a racist and a xenophobe and un-American for even raising these issues, revealed the gap between the two parties and the threat that progressives' "globalist" ideas and open-borders aspirations actually pose. The New Republicanism must be a movement opposed to the progressives' sellout of American sovereignty, of America's historical uniqueness. It must be unapologetic in its patriotism and in its commitment to rebuilding America economically and militarily. Third, the New Republicanism must show its contempt for a political correctness that denies the virtues of America's culture, which is founded on individual rights and equality before the law. It must oppose progressive "multiculturalism," which seeks to replace this culture with anti-American hierarchies of gender, class, and race.

To begin to stop the progressive juggernaut, Republicans must take the political wars to the progressive bases of power. Taking political agendas out of America's classrooms must become a priority. It is unconscionable that K–12 children should be indoctrinated—at taxpayers' expense—in the anti-American prejudices of the political left. It is an outrage that universities have purged conservatives from their faculties and reading lists and that conservative speakers should require bodyguards and campus security to ensure their safety when they speak. It is unacceptable that universities should recognize and fund groups that obstruct speakers and harass conservative students.

Republican legislators can begin to restore classical liberal values to universities by making intellectual and political diversity elements of all diversity programs. But the centerpiece of a true reform of education from the K–12 schools to the college level must be the voucherizing of all American public education. Education tax dollars should be put directly into the hands of every American parent to allow them to choose the school that will teach their children. Trump laid the groundwork for this in his Gettysburg address, promising a "School Choice and Education Opportunity Act," which would redirect education dollars and give to parents "the right to send their kid to the public, private, charter, magnet, religious or home school of their choice."[2] The US Department of Education should be restructured to administer the vouchers and its other powers removed. These measures will take the power away from bureaucrats at the federal and local levels and put it in the hands of the people.

Government unions are blatant conflicts of interest and a corrupting force in the body politic. This is particularly true at the local level, where the unions' power to elect their employers and hold elected officials hostage has encumbered state and municipal budgets with unsustainable burdens. It is also true at the federal level, where government unions are able to block necessary reforms and use their political influence to advance the interests of their members over the interests of the public they are supposed to serve. This is especially tragic in our inner-city public schools, which are failing because the teacher unions place the interests of their adult members over the needs of the children.

The shadow political universe of tax-exempt foundations and advocacy groups, which is overwhelmingly on the left, should be the focus of congressional scrutiny and reform. Multibillion-dollar trusts that exist in perpetuity and are accountable to no one while they invest massive funds in social engineering projects constitute a large and growing threat to our democracy. Their empowerment of radical, violence-inciting groups like Black Lives Matter has obvious and disturbing political implications. When a handful of powerful foundations can put $100 million in the hands of a group whose "protests" result in millions of dollars in civic damage, injuries, and fatalities to ordinary citizens; assassinations of police officers; and a resulting spike in homicides in the cities affected, the implications for social order and for future political conflicts are deeply disturbing. Congressional Republicans should be on the case, drafting legislation to address this.

Black Lives Matter is part of the Democrats' strategy to keep 90 percent of African American voters casting their ballots for the party every four years, after which they can safely ignore them. This is a vital Democratic base that Republicans have ceded for far too long. In a speech in Charlotte, Trump offered a new deal for Black America:

> Today I want to talk about how to grow the African-American middle class, and to provide a new deal for Black America. That deal is grounded in three promises: safe communities, great education, and high-paying jobs. I have a message for all the doubters in Washington: America's future belongs to the dreamers, not the cynics. And it's time to extend that dream

> to every African-American citizen in this country. African-American citizens have sacrificed so much for this nation. They have fought and died in every war since the Revolution, and from the pews and the picket lines they have lifted up the conscience of our country in the long march for Civil Rights. Yet, too many African-Americans have been left behind.[3]

A new deal for African Americans would lay siege to the Democrats' most secure and important stronghold. Trump continued: "The Democrats have run our inner cities for fifty, sixty, seventy years or more. They've run the school boards, the city councils, the mayor's offices, and the congressional seats. Their policies have failed, and they've failed miserably. They've trapped children in failing government schools, and opposed school choice at every turn."[4]

This is the gauntlet that Republicans must throw down to the Democrats to break their stranglehold on America's large urban centers, which have delivered states to them with large electoral vote totals, thus creating the electoral "lock" that confronts Republicans every four years.

If this election season did nothing else, it served to dramatize Trump's claim that "the system is rigged," and the level of unchecked corruption is greater than anyone thought. The FBI is already engaged in a criminal investigation of the Clinton Foundation. But why were the Clintons and their associates able to conduct such an operation for so long without an investigation? Why was Secretary of State Clinton able to take large sums of money from foreign governments throughout her tenure without anyone asking what's going on?

In his Gettysburg address, Trump promised several measures designed to end the influence-peddling of government officials, including "a constitutional amendment to impose term limits on all members of Congress; a 5-year-ban on White House and congressional officials becoming lobbyists after they leave government service; a lifetime ban on White House officials lobbying on behalf of a foreign government; and a complete ban on foreign lobbyists raising money for American elections."[5]

The IRS must be investigated and reformed to prevent Democrats from using it to suppress the opinions of their political opponents. IRS officials who participated in the effort to prevent conservative think tanks and advocacy groups from tax exemptions available to their liberal adversaries should be prosecuted. During the Obama administration, the Justice Department became a political arm (and fixer) for the White House. Attorney General Holder added 130 new DOJ lawyers during his tenure, every single one of whom was a leftist or a far leftist. The department's role in serving partisan political agendas while pretending to enforce the law has been well documented.[6] Reform of a Justice Department that has been stacked with left-wing operatives and no longer operates on the principle that its mission is to impartially enforce the law must be a first order of business. The corruption of an FBI investigation at the highest level, as revealed during the 2016 campaign, severely damages the respect for the law that is crucial to holding a society together. The facts are clear. Secretary of State Hillary Clinton knowingly violated multiple provisions of the Espionage Act. She then obstructed justice and perjured herself to cover up her crimes. She lied to Congress and to the public—as only the guilty do—to cover up her violations of the law. But she incurred no legal consequences. How damaging is *that* to the rule of law and to the core idea that ours is a government of laws and not of individuals who can get away with anything if they have the right friends?

In regard to respecting the law, the obscenity of Sanctuary cities that have pledged to subvert the nation's security has to be ended. In his "Contract with the American Voter," Trump promised to "withdraw all federal funding from Sanctuary Cities."[7] That's all well and good, but it does not go nearly far enough. Sanctuary Cities are seditious threats to the safety of all Americans. Elected officials who pledge to break the law and then act to do so need to be removed from office and prosecuted. So-called civil disobedience cannot be an option for officers of the law. State governments that are not in the hands of progressives need to act to remedy this situation and provide an object lesson in what it means to be patriotic officials in a law-abiding society.

13

A Party for All the People

DONALD TRUMP IS THE first Republican to have put working Americans at the center of his appeals. In his "Contract with the American Voter," he promised that on day one, he would take the following seven actions to protect American workers:

> First, I will announce my intention to renegotiate NAFTA or withdraw from the deal under Article 2205; second, I will announce our withdrawal from the Trans-Pacific Partnership; third, I will direct my Secretary of the Treasury to label China a currency manipulator; fourth, I will direct the Secretary of Commerce and U.S. Trade Representative to identify all foreign trading abuses that unfairly impact American workers

> and direct them to use every tool under American and international law to end those abuses immediately; fifth, I will lift the restrictions on the production of $50 trillion dollars' worth of job producing American energy reserves, including shale, oil, natural gas and clean coal; sixth, lift the Obama-Clinton roadblocks and allow vital energy infrastructure projects, like the Keystone Pipeline, to move forward; seventh, cancel billions in payments to U.N. climate change programs and use the money to fix America's water and environmental infrastructure.[1]

Trump is actually the first Republican to speak to all Americans: to the Evangelical and LGBTQ communities; to blacks and whites; to Democrats, Bernie Sanders supporters, and Republicans. While the political battle we face is divisive, it is a battle based not on immutable characteristics like race and gender, not on identity, but on ideas, and specifically the ideas of America's founding fathers and against the progressive assault on those ideas. Not all Democrats understand the implications of their party's commitments, since their leaders are adept at camouflaging them or, like Hillary and Obama, brazenly lying about them. Not all Democrats are progressives, though it is difficult to discern a leader of the Democratic Party who is not. Since the Republican vision is a vision not of identities in conflict but of a diverse society of individuals who are free and equal before the law, its appeal is universal and inclusive. People who disagree politically can come together and compromise over their differences.

"I will fight for every neglected part of this nation—and I will fight to bring us all together as One American People," Trump told an audience in Miami. "Imagine what our country could accomplish if we started working together as One People, under One God, saluting One American Flag. It is time to break with the bitter failures of the past, and to embrace a new, inclusive and prosperous American future. Jobs will return, incomes will rise, and new factories will come rushing back to our shores. Once more, we will have a government of, by and for the people. We Will Make America Prosperous Again. We Will Make America Strong Again. And We Will Make America Great Again."[2]

Trump's inclusiveness is all but overlooked by a biased national media, which worked hard during the campaign to do the Democrats' dirty work and portray him as a bigot, a misogynist, an Islamophobe, a xenophobe, and in general, deplorable. Also overlooked, and not only by the left-wing media but by conservatives as well, was the irony that the overarching theme of Trump's campaign—as it should be of all Republican campaigns—was hope and change: "All I see everywhere I travel in this nation is untapped potential waiting to be realized. If we unlock the potential of this country, no dream is outside of our reach. If we stop believing in our failed politicians and start believing in ourselves then anything—anything—is possible. I'm asking you to dream big, to push for bold change, and to believe in a movement powered by our love for each other and our love for our country. That is how we will truly make America great again."[3]

Donald Trump will have to be president of all the American people, and this will inevitably put restraints on the aggressiveness he displayed in the campaign. Well and good. But the resistance to him and his policies will be just as great and probably greater. There will be protest/riots in the streets and in front of the White House. There will be the same "gotcha" politics, the same lies and slanders, the same distortions from the left and its media as in the election campaign. Every misstep will be amplified, every adversity exaggerated. And the agenda will be as it was during the campaign: to destroy him and to destroy everybody who supports him. The good news is that the election showed that millions of Americans see through the distortions and are not swayed by the slanders. The good news is that millions upon millions of Americans understand the nature of the battles and the stakes of the war. And their understanding and determination will change the Republican Party and transform it into a force that wants to win.

Conclusion

THE BATTLE PLAN: THE FIRST 100 DAYS

EVERY FIGHT REQUIRES A battle plan. Stopping the progressive crusade to systematically dismantle the principles of liberty and the Constitution will not be easy. Ronald Reagan wisely told us that freedom is never more than a generation away from extinction—and that means failure is not an option.

Only by understanding the ideology of progressives and their true agenda, only by understanding that they view the acquisition of power as a self-justifying goal regardless of the means used to acquire it, can defenders of American values hope to prevail.

We have offered the agenda, the order of battle, to halt the left's march to fundamentally transform—and ultimately extinguish—the shining city on a hill, the beacon of freedom that is America.

The First 100 Days of the Trump Presidency

EXECUTIVE ORDERS

On day one, Trump will sign at least 20 executive orders to undo the illegal subversion of the Constitution and its balance of powers undertaken by former president Barack Obama. Among them are the following:

TPP, RIP—Voters rejected the Trans-Pacific Partnership and the mainstream consensus on trade and immigration. President Trump will listen to the voice of the people and negotiate new deals.

Restore Guantanamo—Democrats are uncomfortable fighting the war on terror. They are in denial about our radical Islamic enemies and want to treat terrorists as ordinary criminals, affording them the rights of American citizens. They want to read them their Miranda rights and provide them with opportunities to convert and recruit other prisoners. The detention facility at Guantanamo is one of the most carefully monitored incarceration facilities of its kind in the world, and it should be maintained as an essential tool in America's war on terror.

Relocate America's Embassy in Israel—Israel is the front-line state in the war against Islamic terrorism. The capital of Israel always has been and always will be Jerusalem. It is time to stand up for our one staunch ally in the Middle East and recognize that there can be no peace as long as Palestinians support terror and deny Israel's right to exist.

Keystone XL and Drilling on Federal Lands—President Trump will promote US energy independence to thwart the left's agenda to make America dependent on global partners whose heartfelt hope is to undermine America.

Nixing Amnesty—President Trump should fire the current left-wing Justice Department officials, instruct the new attorney general to end the corruption, and resume enforcement of US immigration laws, including immediate deportation of the estimated two to three million illegals with criminal records.

Defund Sanctuary Cities and Prosecute Officials Who Support Them—Some 340 jurisdictions have absolved themselves from cooperating with federal authorities on the enforcement of US immigration law. President Trump, in return, should declare those jurisdictions no longer eligible to receive at least some streams of federal funding. The Justice Department should look into prosecuting city officials who defend their pledge to ignore federal immigration laws and to refuse to cooperate with the Department of Homeland Security.

JUDICIAL APPOINTMENTS

Supreme Court—President Trump must act on his pledge to nominate a conservative justice willing to follow in the footsteps of the late, great Justice Antonin Scalia. The key litmus test for Senate confirmation should be the recognition that the Constitution's clear meaning must not be distorted to conform to a leftist agenda.

Other Judicial Appointments–Because Democrats lowered the threshold for ordinary judicial confirmations to just 51 votes in the Senate, Republicans must cast off Democratic stonewalling and exhibit the will to quickly fill all vacancies in the federal judiciary with justices who favor Constitutional literalism over progressives' "socially desirable" outcomes. This will finally begin to redress the imbalance in judges brought on by eight long years of Obama appointees.

RULES AND REGULATIONS

Countermand the Affordable Care Act–The expansion of the imperial presidency under President Obama means much of what passes for law in this country are actually federal regulations. President Trump has promised to order the federal bureaucracy to move quickly to cancel them. Nowhere is this more urgent than in the case of the Affordable Care Act. While he's awaiting congressional legislation to replace Obamacare, Trump should order the US Department of Health and Human Services to begin dismantling it. One alternative is to make it easier for states to establish their own alternative health care systems. It's also time to stop the federal effort to recruit new enrollees into a health care regime that, based on narrowing provider bases and spiraling premiums, is already imploding.

Attack IRS Malfeasance–The IRS has continued to add insult to injury with its persecution of conservative nonprofit organizations long after Obama apparatchik Lois Lerner left government service. To restore a culture of law and order in the federal government, the Trump administration should launch a wholesale investigation into those responsible at every level of the IRS bureaucracy, with penalties up to and including criminal prosecution for those who played ball with the Obama administration's push to wield the agency as a political weapon against its rivals.

Challenge EPA Overreach—President-elect Trump has promised to "cancel" the Paris climate-change deal that threatens to ensnare US autonomy in a web of international accords that blatantly favor India and the Chinese. Also look for him to declare the EPA's "Clean Power Plan"—a scheme to weaken the energy sector by limiting the carbon emissions of US power plants—to be null and void. That plan is already frozen by an order of the US Supreme Court, pending a judicial review.

New Deal for Black America and the Inner Cities—Trump must act quickly on his promise of a "New Deal for Black America"—to make inner cities "safe," to increase educational opportunities for their children, and to provide jobs. Republicans at the state levels must begin to challenge progressives in their political powerbase in the inner cities. Democrats' monopoly control of America's inner cities is actually their Achilles' heel. The best way to break that monopoly is to use Department of Education funding to pay for scholarships and vouchers to help parents select the public or private school of their choice. Eliminating the public-sector unions' monopoly on education will expose the left's pretense of social justice for the cruel sham it is. Trump may be able to accomplish some items on his own, but he has called for a "School Choice and Education Opportunity Act" to restructure the Department of Education to facilitate, rather than impede, the implementation of school choice.

Obamacare's Replacement—House Speaker Paul Ryan has let it be known that two pieces of legislation are almost ready to be introduced. In January, President Obama vetoed legislation that would have repealed the Affordable Care Act. It also would have defunded Planned Parenthood. Now, with a member of their own party in the White House, congressional Republicans must figure out a way to preserve the popular aspects of health care reform—coverage for preexisting conditions, for example—while extricating the federal government's sticky fingers from the one-sixth of the US economy that health care represents. Much of this work can be done through the "reconciliation" maneuver that was originally used to pass the bill, meaning just 51 votes in the Senate can put the bill on the president's desk.

Tax Reform—Reducing the share of the monies the federal government confiscates from its citizens is politically toxic for Democrats. So the absurdly high US corporate tax rate of 35 percent, the highest in the world among developed nations, has gone unaddressed year after year. With Republicans in charge across the board, that must quickly change. House and Senate leaders must cut US corporate taxes to repatriate the estimated $2.5 trillion in profits that American-based companies have simply parked overseas, where the capital is lost to the US economy. On the campaign trail, Trump also promised to lower the top marginal rate for individuals to 33 percent. The bottom line: Nothing would do more to stimulate our lagging economy than overhauling a tax code that is both burdensome and unwieldy.

Infrastructure Spending—The last time Congress passed an infrastructure spending bill, most of the money went to pet congressional projects and progressive nostrums such as clean energy. Now Trump wants genuine infrastructure spending to rebuild America's communication and transportation networks. It's part of his plan to "Make America Great Again," but he'll need the support of Congress to make it happen.

To stop the progressive juggernaut dead in its tracks, Republicans must challenge the base of power progressives depend on by offering genuine opportunities to the disadvantaged urban communities that Democrats have ruled, exploited, and paid lip service to for decades. Restoring law and order, offering school choice, ending the open-borders policy, and rebuilding America's infrastructure will do wonders for an inner-city community that knows liberals have been long on promises and short on delivery.

What matters from this point forward is not what we say but what we do. We must rise up and confront those who no longer believe in America as the exceptional bastion of freedom that it is. Along with Reagan, we must fight to defend liberty in order to bequeath it to the next generation.

Let it not be said we shrank from the great calling of our times: to faithfully defend the "last best hope" of freedom that is the United States.

Notes

INTRODUCTION

1 Larry Paros, "Mourning in America," *Huffington Post*, November 10, 2016, http://www.huffingtonpost.com/larry-paros/mourning-in-america_b_12902508.html.

2 "President Trump: A Colossal Failure for Democracy and Our Terrifying New Reality," *Salon.com*, November 9, 2016, http://www.salon.com/2016/11/09/a-colossal-failure-of-democracy-president-trump-is-almost-certainly-our-terrifying-new-reality/.

3 Josiah Ryan, "'This Was a Whitelash': Van Jones' Take on the Election Results," *CNN*, November 9, 2016, http://www.cnn.com/2016/11/09/politics/van-jones-results-disappointment-cnntv/.

4 Jamelle Bouie, "White Won," *Slate.com*, November 9, 2016, http://www.slate.com/articles/news_and_politics/politics/2016/11/white_won.html.

5 Mark Joseph Stern, "I Am a Gay Jew in Trump's America. And I Am Afraid for My Life," *Slate.com*, November 9, 2016, http://www.slate

.com/blogs/outward/2016/11/09/i_am_a_gay_jew_in_trump_s_america_and_i_am_terrified.html.

Part I: The Adversary

I:2

1 Louis Jacobson, "Mitt Romney Praised Donald Trump's Business Skill in 2012, then Flip-Flopped in 2016," *Politifact*, March 6, 2016, http://www.politifact.com/truth-o-meter/statements/2016/mar/06/mitt-romney/mitt-romney-praised-donald-trumps-business-skill-2/.

2 Eric Bradner and Catherine Treyz, "Romney Implores: Bring down Trump," *CNN*, March 3, 2016, http://www.cnn.com/2016/03/03/politics/mitt-romney-presidential-race-speech/.

3 Yousef Saba, "Jeb Bush: 'No Apology Can Excuse Away Donald Trump's Reprehensible Comments,'" *Politico*, October 7, 2016, http://www.politico.com/story/2016/10/jeb-bush-donald-trump-comments-women-229314#ixzz4NTDMVY7B.

4 Cooper Allen and Fredreka Schouten, "Trump Apologizes for Video Bragging about Groping Women," *USA Today*, October 8, 2016, http://www.usatoday.com/story/news/politics/onpolitics/2016/10/07/trump-washington-post-women-billy-bush-video/91743992/.

5 "BFFs Bill Clinton, George W. Bush Talk about Hillary, Jeb, and Their Friendship," *The Week*, July 9, 2015, http://theweek.com/speedreads/565703/bffs-bill-clinton-george-w-bush-talk-about-hillary-jeb-friendship.

6 "Limbaugh: GOP Doesn't Want to Win," *Patriot News Daily*, October 12, 2016, http://patriotnewsdaily.com/limbaugh-gop-doesnt-want-to-win/.

I:3

1 Andrew C. McCarthy, "The Problem Is Not the Presidential Candidates," *PJ Media*, October 17, 2016, https://pjmedia.com/andrewmccarthy/2016/10/17/the-problem-is-not-the-presidential-candidates/2/.

2 Lauren Windsor, "Caught on Tape: What Mitch McConnell Complained about to a Roomful of Billionaires (Exclusive)," *The Nation*, August 26, 2014, https://www.thenation.com/article/

caught-tape-what-mitch-mcconnell-complained-about-roomful-billionaires-exclusive/.

3 McCarthy, "The Problem Is Not the Presidential Candidates."

4 I have previously written an entire book devoted to providing a response, which can be read as a supplement to this one: *Take No Prisoners: The Battle Plan for Defeating the Left* (Washington, DC: Regnery, 2014).

I:4

1 Phil Gramm, "Where Clinton Will Take ObamaCare," *Wall Street Journal*, October 17, 2016, http://www.wsj.com/articles/where-clinton-will-take-obamacare-1476746073.

2 Angie Drobnic Holan, "In Context: Hillary Clinton and the 'Basket of Deplorables,'" *Politifact*, September 11, 2016, http://www.politifact.com/truth-o-meter/article/2016/sep/11/context-hillary-clinton-basket-deplorables/.

3 Charlie Spiering, "Hillary Clinton Tries to Smear Donald Trump with KKK Newspaper," *Breitbart*, November 3, 2016, http://www.breitbart.com/2016-presidential-race/2016/11/03/hillary-clinton-kkk-newspaper-endorsed-donald-trump/; Charlie Spiering, "Obama: Donald Trump Would Tolerate Klan If Elected President," *Breitbart*, November 3, 2016, http://www.breitbart.com/2016-presidential-race/2016/11/03/obama-donald-trump-will-tolerate-klu-klux-klan-elected-president/.

I:5

1 "Read the Full Transcript of the Second Presidential Debate between Hillary Clinton and Donald Trump," *Fortune*, October 9, 2016, http://fortune.com/2016/10/09/presidential-debate-read-transcript-donald-trump-hillary-clinton.

2 Jack Cashill, *You Lie! The Evasions, Omissions, Fabrications, Frauds, and Outright Falsehoods of Barack Obama* (Kindle Edition, Broadside e-books, 2014).

3 John Nolte, "Bombshell: 'Washington Post' Confirms Hillary Clinton Started the Birther Movement," *Breitbart*, September 26, 2015, http://www.breitbart.com/big-journalism/2015/09/26/washington-post-confirms-hillary-clinton-started-the-birther-movement/.

4 Larry Elder, "Is America Racist?," *PragerU*, January 18, 2016, https://www.prageru.com/courses/race-relations/america-racist.
5 Ibid.

I:6

1 Jim Hoft, "Rumblings: Top Paul Ryan Advisor Leaked Trump Sex Talk Tape to WaPo (Updated)," *The Gateway Pundit*, October 10, 2016, http://www.thegatewaypundit.com/2016/10/report-top-paul-ryan-advisor-leaked-trump-sex-talk-tape-wapo/.

I:7

1 The analysis of Alinsky that follows is drawn from David Horowitz, "Rules for Revolution," in *The Left in Power: Clinton to Obama*, volume 7 of *The Black Book of the American Left* (Washington, DC: Regnery, 2016), chapter 4.
2 Stanley Kurtz, *Radical-in-Chief: Barack Obama and the Untold Story of American Socialism* (New York: Threshold, 2010).
3 Saul Alinsky, *Rules for Radicals: A Pragmatic Primer for Realistic Radicals* (New York: Vintage), 3.
4 Ibid., xiii.
5 Ibid., 10–11.
6 Ibid., 24–25.
7 Ibid., 25.
8 Ryan Lizza, "The Agitator," *The New Republic*, March 9, 2007.
9 Ibid., March 19, 2007.
10 Peter Slevin, "For Clinton and Obama, a Common Ideological Touchstone," *Washington Post*, March 25, 2007, http://www.washingtonpost.com/wp-dyn/content/article/2007/03/24/AR2007032401152.html.

Part II: The Agenda

II:1

1 Saul Alinsky, *Rules for Radicals: A Pragmatic Primer for Realistic Radicals* (New York: Vintage), xix.
2 Ibid., xxiii.
3 Angie Drobnic Holan, "Lie of the Year: 'If You like Your Health Care Plan, You Can Keep It,'" *Politifact*, December 12, 2013, http://www

.politifact.com/truth-o-meter/article/2013/dec/12/lie-year-if-you-like-your-health-care-plan-keep-it/.

4 "Joe Wilson Proved Right: Obama Did 'Lie' on Illegal Alien Health Coverage," *Conservative Review*, February 8, 2016, https://www.conservativereview.com/commentary/2016/02/joe-wilson-right-obama-lied-on-illegals-and-healthcare.

5 "GRUBER: Lack of Transparency Is a Huge Political Advantage," YouTube video, posted by "AmericanCommitment," November 7, 2014, https://www.youtube.com/watch?v=G790p0LcgbI; "AHEC Agenda," University of Pennsylvania Leonard Davis Institute of Health Economics, Fourth Annual Health Economics Conference, October 17 and 18, 2013, Wharton School, University of Pennsylvania, http://ldi.upenn.edu/ahec2013/agenda.

6 "Issues: Health Care," *HillaryClinton.com*, https://www.hillaryclinton.com/issues/health-care/.

II:2

1 *The Federalist Papers*: No. 47, http://avalon.law.yale.edu/18th_century/fed47.asp.

2 Yuval Levin and Ramesh Ponnuru, "Hillary Is an Embodiment of the Left's Disdain for Democracy," *National Review*, September 26, 2016, http://www.nationalreview.com/article/440362/hillary-clinton-presidential-campaign-threatens-america-republican-system.

3 These words were spoken by Jonathan Gruber, a principal architect of Obamacare. "GRUBER: Lack of Transparency Is a Huge Political Advantage," YouTube video, posted by "AmericanCommitment," November 7, 2014, https://www.youtube.com/watch?v=G790p0LcgbI.

4 Jonathan Easley, "Sanders: Climate Change Still Greatest Threat to National Security," *The Hill*, November 14, 2015, http://thehill.com/policy/energy-environment/260184-sanders-climate-change-still-greatest-threat-to-national-security.

5 "Issues: Climate Change," *HillaryClinton.com*, https://www.hillaryclinton.com/issues/climate/.

II:3

1 "Obama: 'Fundamentally Transforming the United States of America' Long Version," YouTube video, posted by "jbranstetter04," May 20, 2011, https://www.youtube.com/watch?v=KrefKCaV8m4.

2 Michael Kelly, "Saint Hillary," *New York Times*, May 23, 1993, http://www.nytimes.com/1993/05/23/magazine/saint-hillary.html?pagewanted=all.

3 "2016 Democratic Party Platform," *American Presidency Project*, July 21, 2016, http://www.presidency.ucsb.edu/ws/index.php?pid=117717.

4 John Fonte, "Transformers," *Claremont Institute*, October 19, 2016, http://www.claremont.org/crb/basicpage/transformers/.

5 "2016 Democratic Party Platform."

II:4

1 John Fonte, "Transformers," *Claremont Institute*, October 19, 2016, http://www.claremont.org/crb/basicpage/transformers/.

2 Tom Tancredo, "Obama Invites 18.7 Million Immigrants to Avoid Oath of Allegiance, Pledge to Defend America," *Breitbart*, June 25, 2016, http://www.breitbart.com/big-government/2016/06/25/obama-invites-18-7-million-immigrants-avoid-oath-allegiance-pledge-defend-america/.

3 Ian Schwartz, "Trump: 'We Don't Have a Country without a Border,'" *RealClear Politics*, July 24, 2015, http://www.realclearpolitics.com/video/2015/07/24/trump_we_dont_have_a_country_without_a_border.html.

4 This came to light in the WikiLeaks documents.

5 Fonte, "Transformers."

6 David Horowitz, *Unholy Alliance: Radical Islam and the American Left* (Washington, DC: Regnery, 2004), 196–97.

7 "Draft Resolution," ACLU, https://www.aclu.org/other/draft-resolution.

8 "Rep. Louie Gohmert: The Islamist Enemy Within," *Frontpage Mag*, May 16, 2013, http://www.frontpagemag.com/fpm/189800/rep-louie-gohmert-islamist-enemy-within-frontpagemagcom.

9 "Al-Qaeda: Declarations & Acts of War," *The Heritage Foundation*, http://www.heritage.org/research/projects/enemy-detention/al-qaeda-declarations.

10 "Muslim Opinion Polls: A Tiny Minority of Extremists?," *The Religion of Peace*, http://www.thereligionofpeace.com/pages/articles/opinion-polls.aspx; "Beliefs and Allegiances of Muslims," *Discover the Networks*, http://www.discoverthenetworks.org/viewSubCategory.asp?id=2454.

11 "Verse (8:12): English Translation," *The Quranic Arabic Corpus*, http://corpus.quran.com/translation.jsp?chapter=8&verse=12.

12 Associated Press, "Analysis: Obama Telling Mubarak: Time to Go," *CBS News*, February 5, 2011, http://www.cbsnews.com/news/analysis-obama-telling-mubarak-time-to-go/.

13 Charles Krauthammer, "How Obama Swindled Americans on Iran," *National Review*, September 10, 2015, http://www.nationalreview.com/article/423845/iran-deal-obama-resolution.

14 Donna Rachel Edmunds, "UN's Human Rights Council Condemns Israel More than Rest of World Combined," *Breitbart*, June 25, 2015, http://www.breitbart.com/london/2015/06/25/uns-human-rights-council-condemns-israel-more-than-rest-of-world-combined/; "Issue 589: UN Watch Testifies in U.S. Congress: UN Human Rights Council Has Turned into Frankenstein," *UN Watch*, May 19, 2016, http://www.unwatch.org/issue-589-un-watch-testifies-u-s-congress-un-human-rights-council-turned-frankenstein/.

15 Eric Lieberman, "Obama Admin Wants to Surrender US Control over Internet to Global Bureaucracy," *The Daily Caller*, September 24, 2016, http://dailycaller.com/2016/09/24/obama-admin-wants-to-surrender-us-control-over-internet-to-global-bureaucracy/.

16 "Ginsburg to Egyptians: I Wouldn't Use U.S. Constitution as a Model," *FOX News*, February 6, 2012, http://www.foxnews.com/politics/2012/02/06/ginsburg-to-egyptians-wouldnt-use-us-constitution-as-model.html.

17 "The Constitution of the Republic of South Africa," http://www.gov.za/documents/constitution/constitution-republic-south-Africa-1996-1.

18 James Madison, *The Federalist* No. 10, November 22, 1787, http://www.constitution.org/fed/federa10.htmto.

19 "Full Transcript: Third 2016 Presidential Debate," *Politico*, October 20, 2016, http://www.politico.com/story/2016/10/full-transcript-third-2016-presidential-debate-230063.

20 "Campaign Finance Reform (McCain-Feingold)," *Discover the Networks*, http://www.discoverthenetworks.org/viewSubCategory.asp?id=456.

21 Benjamin Oreskes, "Clinton Pledges Constitutional Amendment to Overturn Citizens United Ruling," *Politico*, July 16, 2016, http://www.politico.com/story/2016/07/hillary-clinton-citizens-united-225658#ixzz4OtlMAFTp.

22 For a book on the subject by a liberal Democrat, see Kirsten Powers, *The Silencing: How the Left Is Killing Free Speech* (Washington, DC: Regnery, 2015).

23 Mitchell Langbert, Anthony J. Quain, and Daniel B. Klein, "Faculty Voter Registration in Economics, History, Journalism, Law, and Psychology," *Character Issues* 13, no. 3 (September 2016): 422–51, https://econjwatch.org/articles/faculty-voter-registration-in-economics-history-journalism-communications-law-and-psychology.

24 Michael Stratford, "After Calling Trump a Bully, Clinton Campaign Announces Anti-Bullying Plan," *Politico*, October, 27, 2016, http://www.politico.com/story/2016/10/clinton-anti-bullying-plan-230377#ixzz4OPef5SY5.

25 Wikipedia, s.v. "Microaggression Theory," https://en.wikipedia.org/wiki/Microaggression_theory.

26 Josh Hedtke, "California Professors Instructed Not to Say 'America Is the Land of Opportunity,'" *The College Fix*, June 10, 2015, http://www.thecollegefix.com/post/22839/.

27 David Horowitz and Robert Spencer, "Islamophobia: Thought Crime of the Totalitarian Future," *Frontpage Mag*, May 8, 2015, http://www.frontpagemag.com/fpm/256647/islamophobia-thought-crime-totalitarian-future-david-horowitz.

28 Wajahat Ali, Eli Clifton, Matthew Duss, Lee Fang, Scott Keyes, and Faiz Shakir, *Fear, Inc.: The Roots of the Islamophobia Network in America*, Center for American Progress, August 2011, https://cdn.americanprogress.org/wp-content/uploads/issues/2011/08/pdf/islamophobia.pdf.

Part III: The Strategy

III:2

1 Jim Hoft, "List of Debunked Groper Allegations by Corrupt Media against Donald Trump," *The Gateway Pundit*, October 15, 2016, http://www.thegatewaypundit.com/2016/10/list-debunked-groper-allegations-corrupt-media-donald-trump/.

2 Tyler Durden, "Huffington Post Ends Editor's Note Calling Trump 'Serial Liar, Rampant Xenophobe, Racist, Misogynist,'" *Zero Hedge*, November 9, 2016, http://www.zerohedge.com/news/2016-11-09/huffington-post-ends-editors-note-calling-trump-serial-liar-rampant-xenophobe-racist.

III:3

1. "Trump Offers 'New Deal' to African-Americans in Charlotte," *Fix This Nation*, October 27, 2016, http://www.fixthisnation.com/conservative-breaking-news/trump-offers-new-deal-to-african-americans-in-charlotte/.
2. "Donald Trump Calls for Inner City School Choice in Speech to Values Voters," *DonaldJTrump.com*, September 9, 2016, https://www.donaldjtrump.com/press-releases/donald-trump-calls-for-inner-city-school-choice-in-speech-to-values-voters.
3. Kat Kane, "Democrats Just Adopted the Most Progressive Platform in Party History: 5 Things You Should Know," *HillaryClinton.com*, July 25, 2016, https://www.hillaryclinton.com/feed/democrats-just-adopted-the-most-progressive-platform-in-party-history-5-things-you-should-know/.
4. "2016 Democratic Party Platform," *DemConvention.com*, July 21, 2016, https://www.demconvention.com/wp-content/uploads/2016/07/Democratic-Party-Platform-7.21.16-no-lines.pdf.
5. Ibid.
6. David Horowitz and Liz Blaine, "Rules for Revolution Applied," *The Black Book of the American Left*, vol. 7: *The Left in Power: Clinton to Obama* (Washington, DC: Regnery, 2016).
7. Heather MacDonald, *The War on Cops: How the New Attack on Law and Order Makes Everyone Less Safe* (New York: Encounter, 2016).
8. Daniel Greenfield, "The 131 Black Men Murdered by Black Lives Matter," *Frontpage Mag*, October 25, 2016, http://www.frontpagemag.com/fpm/264587/131-black-men-murdered-black-lives-matter-daniel-greenfield.
9. Adelle Nazarian, "Black Lives Matter Accuses Police of 'Genocide' at UC Irvine," *Breitbart*, October 10, 2016, http://www.breitbart.com/california/2016/10/10/black-lives-matter-accuses-police-of-genocide-at-uc-irvine/.
10. Heather MacDonald, "The Myths of Black Lives Matter," *Wall Street Journal*, July 9, 2016, http://www.wsj.com/articles/the-myths-of-black-lives-matter-1468087453.
11. Wikipedia, s.v. "Statistics of Incarcerated African-American Males," https://en.wikipedia.org/wiki/Statistics_of_incarcerated_African-American_males.
12. See Heather MacDonald, *Are Cops Racist?* (Lanham, MD: Ivan R. Dee, 2010).

13 Wikipedia, s.v. "Race and Crime in the United States," https://en.wikipedia.org/wiki/Race_and_crime_in_the_United_States.
14 "National Database of Non-White Elected Officials," *The Gender and Multi-Cultural Leadership Project*, http://www.gmcl.org/database.htm.
15 "'We Are Not Cured': Obama Discusses Racism in America with Marc Maron," *NPR*, June 22, 2015, http://www.npr.org/sections/thetwo-way/2015/06/22/416476377/we-are-not-cured-obama-discusses-racism-in-america-with-marc-maron.

III:4

1 Patricia Zengerle, "Democrats Charge Republicans with 'War on Women' at Convention," *Reuters*, September 4, 2012, http://www.reuters.com/article/2012/09/05/us-usa-campaign-women-idUSBRE88401T20120905.
2 "Mario Cuomo Speaks at the Democratic National Convention," *PBS News Hour*, August 27, 1996, http://www.pbs.org/newshour/bb/politics-july-dec96-cuomo_08-27/.
3 "Hillary Clinton Delivers Remarks on Pay Equity in New York City," *HillaryClinton.com*, https://www.hillaryclinton.com/briefing/updates/2016/04/12/hillary-clinton-delivers-remarks-on-pay-equity-in-new-york-city/.
4 Charlotte Alter, "Hillary Clinton Calls for Closing Wage Gap on Equal Pay Day," *Time.com*, April 12, 2016, http://time.com/4290427/hillary-clinton-equal-pay-day/.
5 "The Equal Pay Act of 1963," US Equal Employment Opportunity Commission, https://www.eeoc.gov/laws/statutes/epa.cfm.
6 Chuck Ross, "Clinton Campaign Found 'Huge' Gender Pay Gap at Clinton Foundation," *The Daily Caller*, October 18, 2016, http://dailycaller.com/2016/10/18/clinton-campaign-found-huge-gender-pay-gap-at-clinton-foundation/#ixzz4OWPjrJEV.

III:5

1 Andrew C. McCarthy, "The Problem Is Not the Presidential Candidates," *PJ Media*, October 17, 2016, https://pjmedia.com/andrewmccarthy/2016/10/17/the-problem-is-not-the-presidential-candidates/2/.
2 Ibid.
3 Ibid.

III:6

1 Emily Ekins, "Millennials Like Socialism—Until They Get Jobs," *Washington Post*, March 24, 2016, http://www.cato.org/publications/commentary/millennials-socialism-until-they-get-jobs?gclid=CjwKEAjwtNbABRCsqO7J0_uJxWYSJAAiVo5LBtU4q_uKdiQT0GDCLl3DQkPDd89V9UhChQwYZjZ7XhoC5gzw_wcB. For more about the Reason-Rupe poll, see Emily Ekins, "Poll: Americans Like Free Markets More than Capitalism and Socialism More than a Govt Managed Economy," *Reason.com*, February 12, 2015, http://reason.com/poll/2015/02/12/poll-americans-like-free-markets-more-th. For the Gallup poll, see Justin McCarthy, "In U.S., Socialist Presidential Candidates Least Appealing," *Gallup.com*, June 22, 2015, http://www.gallup.com/poll/183713/socialist-presidential-candidates-least-appealing.aspx. For more about the Republican exit polls, see CNN: http://www.cnn.com/election/primaries/polls.

2 David Horowitz, *The Professors: The 101 Most Dangerous Academics in America* (Washington, DC: Regnery, 2006); *Indoctrination U.: The Left's War against Academic Freedom* (New York: Encounter, 2009); David Horowitz, *Reforming Our Universities: The Campaign for an Academic Bill of Rights* (Washington, DC: Regnery, 2010); David Horowitz and Jacob Laksin, *One-Party Classroom: How Radical Professors at America's Top Colleges Indoctrinate Students and Undermine Our Democracy* (New York: Crown Forum, 2009).

3 "Preamble to the Constitution of the National Women's Studies Association," *NWSA Journal* 14, no. 1 (2002): xix–xx, https://muse.jhu.edu/article/25340.

4 Wikipedia, s.v. "Intersectionality," https://en.wikipedia.org/wiki/Intersectionality.

5 Horowitz and Laksin, *One-Party Classroom*, 98–100; courses in "empire" taught by equally unqualified professors also abound (223–24).

6 Ibid.

7 Cinnamon Stillwell, "Legitimizing Censorship: 'Islamophobia Studies' at Berkeley," *Jihad Watch*, May 23, 2015, https://www.jihadwatch.org/2015/05/legitimizing-censorship-islamophobia-studies-at-berkeley.

8 Mitchell Langbert, Anthony J. Quain, and Daniel B. Klein, "Faculty Voter Registration in Economics, History, Journalism, Law, and

Psychology," *Character Issues* 13, no. 3 (September 2016): 422–51, https://econjwatch.org/articles/faculty-voter-registration-in-economics-history-journalism-communications-law-and-psychology.

9 "AAUP's 1915 Declaration of Principles," *Campus Watch*, http://www.campus-watch.org/article/id/566. The document was written by two academics, Arthur O. Lovejoy and E. R. A. Seligman.

10 "Obama: 'Fundamentally Transforming the United States of America' Long Version," YouTube video, posted by "jbranstetter04," May 20, 2011, https://www.youtube.com/watch?v=KrefKCaV8m4.

11 Yale diversity mission statement, http://www.yale.edu.

12 Peter Van Voorhis, "Tales from K-12: How High Schools Indoctrinate Students before They Even Get to College," *The College Fix*, July 5, 2016, http://www.thecollegefix.com/post/28051/.

13 https://www.amazon.com/s/ref=nb_sb_ss_i_4_22?url=search-alias%3Daps&field-keywords=teaching+social+justice+mathematics&sprefix=teaching+social+justic%2Caps%2C214&crid=33ZAHGLPN8IPO.

III:7

1 Valerie Richardson, "Black Lives Matter Cashes in with $100 Million from Liberal Foundations," *The Washington Times*, August 16, 2016, http://www.washingtontimes.com/news/2016/aug/16/black-lives-matter-cashes-100-million-liberal-foun/.

2 David Horowitz and Jacob Laksin, "Socialism by Stealth," in *The New Leviathan: How the Left-wing Money Machine Shapes American Politics and Threatens America's Future* (New York: Crown Forum, 2012), chapter 6.

3 For the data, see "Main Funders of the Left," *Discover the Networks*, http://www.discoverthenetworks.org/funders.

4 Horowitz and Laksin, *The New Leviathan*, appendices I–XVI.

5 Ibid., appendices XIV–XVI.

III:8

1 Don Walker, "WSEU Circulating Boycott Letters," *Journal Sentinel*, March 30, 2011, http://www.jsonline.com/blogs/news/118910229.html.

2 Bill Glauber, "Woman Charged with Email Threats," *Journal Sentinel*, March 31, 2011, http://archive.jsonline.com/blogs/news/119023079.html.

3 Deroy Murdock, "Death Threats by the Dozens in Wisconsin," *National Review*, March 18, 2011, http://www.nationalreview.com/article/262428/death-threats-dozens-wisconsin-deroy-murdock.

4 Don Walker, "State Says Damage to Marble at Capitol Could Hit $7.5 Million," *Journal Sentinel*, March 3, 2011, http://www.jsonline.com/blogs/news/117340918.html.

5 Ibid.

6 Matthew Vadum, *Government Unions: How They Rob Taxpayers, Terrorize Workers and Threaten Our Democracy*, a publication of the David Horowitz Freedom Center, 2012.

III:9

1 Tyler Durden, "Doug Band to John Podesta: 'If This Story Gets Out, We Are Screwed,'" *Zero Hedge*, October 30, 2016, http://www.zerohedge.com/news/2016-10-30/doug-band-john-podesta-if-story-gets-out-we-are-screwed.

2 Ibid.

3 "Huma Abedin," *Discover the Networks*, http://www.discoverthenetworks.org/individualProfile.asp?indid=2556; Lee Stranahan, "Clinton Right Hand Woman Huma Abedin Takes the Stage at Center of Email Scandal," *Breitbart*, October 28, 2016, http://www.breitbart.com/big-government/2016/10/28/clinton-right-hand-woman-huma-abedin-takes-the-stage-at-center-of-email-scandal/.

4 Ed O'Keefe, "John Boehner: Accusations against Huma Abedin 'Pretty Dangerous,'" *Washington Post*, July 19, 2012, https://www.washingtonpost.com/pb/blogs/2chambers/post/john-boehner-accusations-against-huma-abedin-pretty-dangerous/2012/07/19/gJQAeDT6vW_blog.html?outputType=accessibility&nid=menu_nav_accessibilityforscreenreader.

III:10

1 David Goldstein, "Gore's Refrain: 'They're for Powerful; We're for People,'" *Deseret News*, August 5, 2000, http://www.deseretnews

.com/article/775647/Gores-refrain-Theyre-for-powerful-were-for-people.html?pg=all.

2 Jacob Brogan, "The Best, Worst, and Most Embarrassing Lines of the Final Presidential Debate," *Slate.com*, October 19, 2016, http://www.slate.com/blogs/the_slatest/2016/10/19/memorable_lines_of_the_final_presidential_debate.html.

3 Edward L. Ayers, *The Promise of the New South: Life after Reconstruction* (New York: Oxford University Press, 2007), 38.

4 Christopher Caldwell, "The Ideological Divide," *New York Times Book Review*, October 24, 2010.

5 Charles Gasparino, *Bought and Paid For: The Unholy Alliance between Barack Obama and Wall Street* (New York: Sentinel, 2010), 30–31.

III:11

1 Jim Hoft, "Tavis Smiley: On Every Leading Economic Issue Black Americans Have Lost Ground under Obama," *The Gateway Pundit*, January 11, 2016, http://www.thegatewaypundit.com/2016/01/tavis-smiley-on-every-leading-economic-issue-black-americans-have-lost-ground-under-obama-video/.

III:12

1 "Donald J. Trump Contract with the American Voter," *DonaldJTrump.com*, https://assets.donaldjtrump.com/CONTRACT_FOR_THE_VOTER.pdf.

2 Ibid.

3 Tim Hains, "Trump Proposes 'New Deal for Black America' in Charlotte," *RealClear Politics*, October 26, 2016, http://www.realclearpolitics.com/video/2016/10/26/trump_proposes_new_deal_for_black_america_in_charlotte.html.

4 Ibid.

5 "Donald J. Trump Contract with the American Voter."

6 "Eric Holder," *Discover the Networks*, http://www.discoverthenetworks.org/individualProfile.asp?indid=2357.

7 "Donald J. Trump Contract with the American Voter."

III:13

1 “Donald J. Trump Contract with the American Voter,” *DonaldJTrump.com*, https://assets.donaldjtrump.com/CONTRACT_FOR_THE_VOTER.pdf.

2 “Transcript of Donald Trump ‘Our United America’ Speech in Miami . . . ,” *The Conservative Tree House*, September 17, 2016, https://theconservativetreehouse.com/2016/09/17/transcript-of-donald-trump-our-united-america-speech-in-miami/.

3 “Full Speech: Donald Trump Rally in Valley Forge, Pennsylvania (11/1/2016) Trump Obamacare Speech,” Donald Trump Speeches & Rallies, YouTube, https://www.youtube.com/watch?v=DYMjNLoOneQ.

Index